DOGS & PUPPIES

Drawing & Activity Book

Brimming with creative inspiration, how-to projects, and useful information to enrich your everyday life, Quarto Knows is a favorite destination for those pursuing their interests and passions. Visit our site and dig deeper with our books into your area of interest: Quarto Creates, Quarto Cooks, Quarto Homes, Quarto Lives, Quarto Drives, Quarto Explores, Quarto Gifts, or Quarto Kids.

Inspiring | Educating | Creating | Entertaining

© 2004, 2014, 2018 Quarto Publishing Group USA Inc.
Photographs © Shutterstock

First Published in 2018 by Walter Foster Jr., an imprint of The Quarto Group.
6 Orchard Road, Suite 100, Lake Forest, CA 92630, USA.
T (949) 380-7510 **F** (949) 380-7575 **www.QuartoKnows.com**

Walter Foster Jr. titles are also available at discount for retail, wholesale, promotional, and bulk purchase. For details, contact the Special Sales Manager by email at specialsales@quarto.com or by mail at The Quarto Group, Attn: Special Sales Manager, 401 Second Avenue North, Suite 310, Minneapolis, MN 55401 USA.

ISBN: 978-1-63322-666-1

Digital edition published in 2018
eISBN: 978-1-63322-667-8

Illustrated by Robbin Cuddy and Diana Fisher

Printed in China
10 9 8 7 6 5 4 3 2 1

MIX
Paper from responsible sources
FSC
www.fsc.org
FSC® C101537

TABLE OF CONTENTS

TOOLS & MATERIALS

You need to gather only a few simple art supplies before you begin. Start with a drawing pencil and an eraser. Make sure you also have a pencil sharpener! Finish your drawings using your choice of art supplies pictured below, such as markers or paints.

drawing pencil

pencils or crayons

felt-tip markers

sharpener

drawing paper

eraser

paintbrushes

paints

TRACING BASICS

This book has five sheets of blank tracing paper, which you can use to trace the dogs pictured on the pages after them.

tracing paper

With your pencil, draw everything you can see over the pup you're tracing, paying close attention to all the little details. Lift the tracing paper up to see your progress.

GRID METHOD

When using the grid method, don't worry about the drawing as a whole. Focus on copying the lines and shapes of just one small square at a time.

 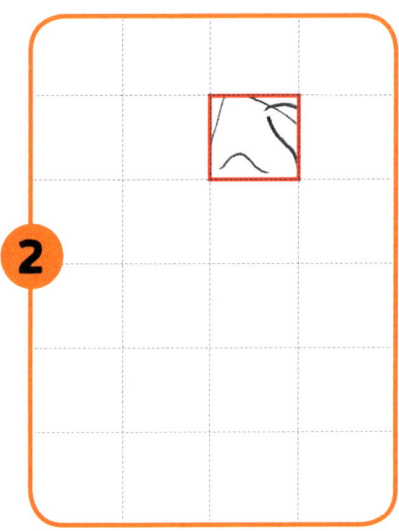 

Choose a square and copy everything into the same square on your blank grid. Make sure you are copying the shapes and lines into the correct spot!

After you've completed all the squares in step one, move on to the next step and keep going!

STEP-BY-STEP METHOD

When using the step-by-step drawing method, you will begin by drawing very basic shapes, such as lines and circles. Each dog with step-by-step instructions has a blank page at the end for you to draw on.

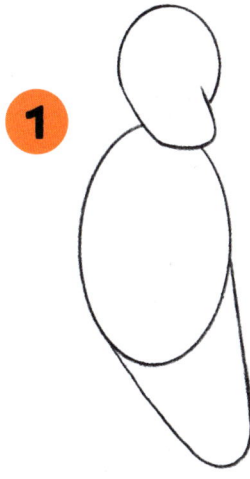

First draw the basic shapes, using light lines that will be easy to erase.

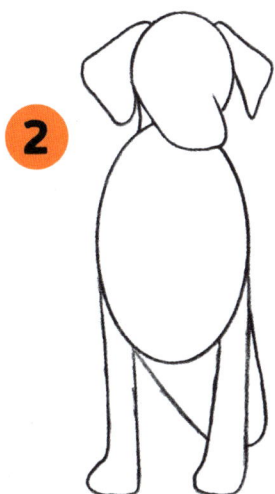

Pay attention to the new lines added in each step.

Erase guidelines and add more detail.

In each new step, add more defining lines.

Take your time adding detail and copying what you see.

Finish your drawing with pencils, markers, paints, or crayons!

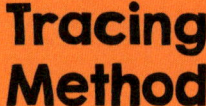

Tracing Method

CHIHUAHUA

These tiny dogs have big eyes, ears, and personalities!

FUN FACT

According to the American Kennel Club (AKC), the Chihuahua is the smallest breed of dog! A full-grown Chihuahua measures from 6 to 9 inches (15 to 23 cm) tall at the shoulder and weighs only 2 to 6 pounds!

Trace your own
Chihuahua on
the transparent
paper.

PUG PUPPY

Adult Pugs have square faces with deep wrinkles. But this Pug is just a pup, so its face is smoother and more rounded.

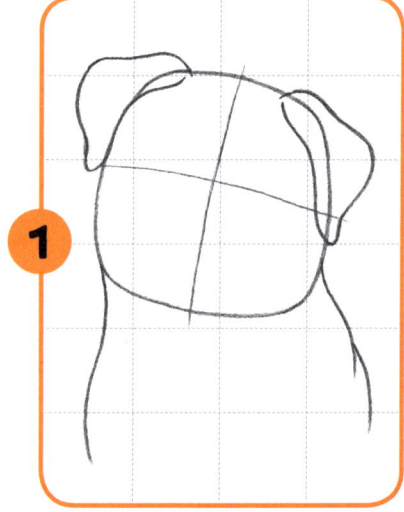

1

2

3

4

5

Copy the lines shown in each step. When you're done with all the steps, you'll have a complete drawing of a Pug. Add details to your drawing with markers, pencils, crayons, or paints.

Step-by-Step

POMERANIAN

Pomeranians have curled tails and thick, fluffy coats that give them an adorable rounded shape.

FUN FACT

Famous "Pom" owners include the composer Mozart and artist Michelangelo.

Follow along, first drawing basic shapes with light pencil lines. Copy the new lines shown in each step, eventually darkening the lines you want to keep and erasing the rest. Finally add details to your drawing with pencils, markers, paints, or crayons.

4

5

6

Draw your own Pomeranian here!

DOG BREED WORD SEARCH

Find and circle the names of different dog breeds hidden in the letters below.

```
Z S A S I B E R I A N H U S K Y W U Y B
S H U X U O G Y S H I H T Z U B H V A O
D G E R M A N S H E P H E R D O I G M R
G O L D E N R E T R I E V E R F P P Y D
T Z D Q P O Y S P R N Q S H E E P B F E
Q T A W O B B X B P O R Z R S S E M V R
Z B L H M R L D D Q E T Z T Y D T C K C
O F M A E O R O Y X O X T L K H V Q L O
K M A K R E Z K O R W V G W T L B Q P L
F K T I A K B B T D M H Q G E B U E R L
M K I T N L U T M T H X T L B I L P O I
P V A A I V V Z J D U O A I D K L H B E
S A N Q A P U G L O W W U B R Z D E T X
F H F N N O J T Q O Y E G N D B O G R Z
E N G L I S H S E T T E R R D I G I E N
B H L Z E C G Q W E I M A R A N E R P Z
Y O R K S H I R E T E R R I E R Y K Q E
V V K J F D C H I H U A H U A R W A B J
```

- ☐ Akita
- ☐ Chihuahua
- ☐ Pomeranian
- ☐ Weimaraner
- ☐ Bloodhound
- ☐ Dalmatian
- ☐ Pug
- ☐ Whippet
- ☐ Border Collie
- ☐ English Setter
- ☐ Rottweiler
- ☐ Yorkshire Terrier
- ☐ Boxer
- ☐ German Shepherd
- ☐ Shih Tzu
- ☐ Bulldog
- ☐ Golden Retriever
- ☐ Siberian Husky

16

Answers on page 64.

DINNER TIME!

Help this pup find its food!

START

FINISH

Answers on page 64.

OLD ENGLISH SHEEPDOG

A shaggy Sheepdog might look like just a big, cuddly ball of fur, but underneath all that hair is a strong body.

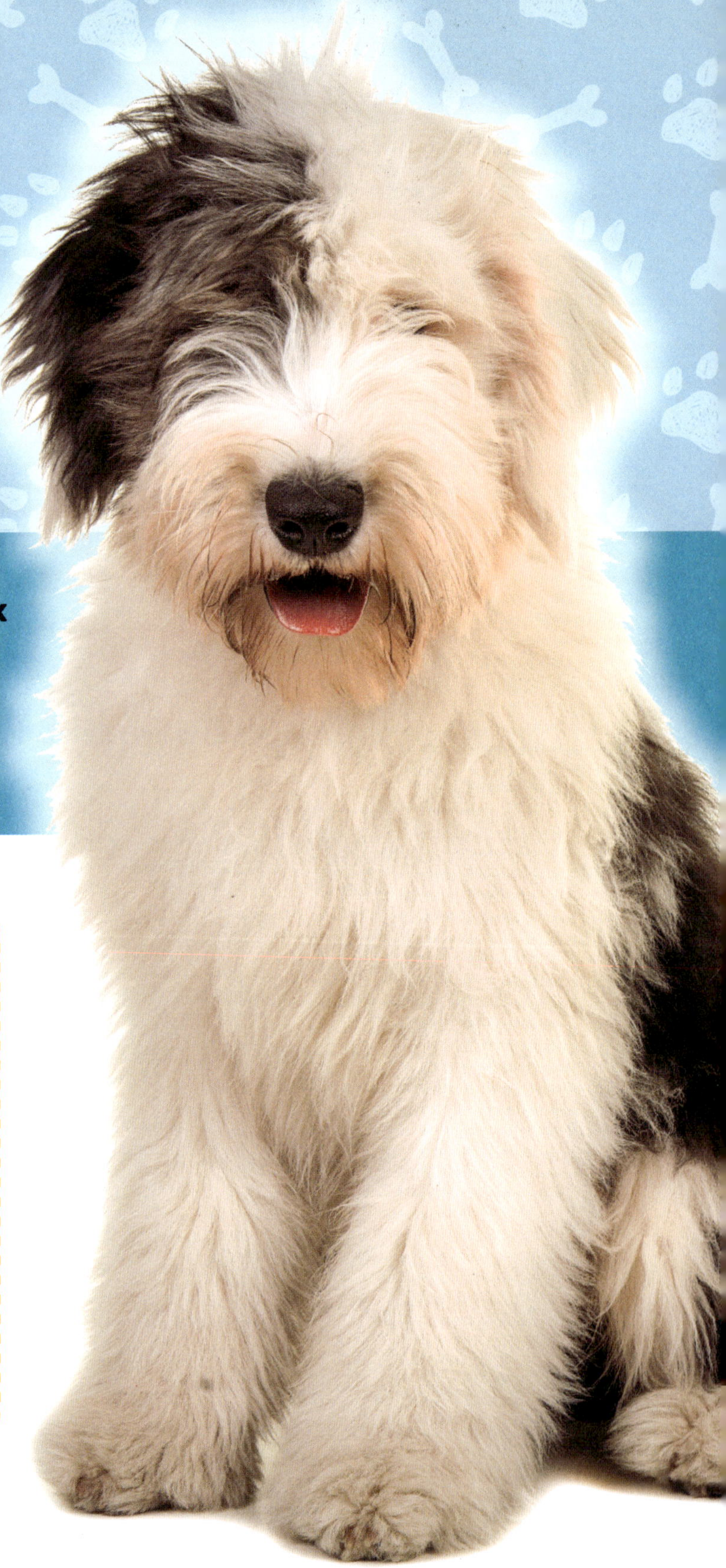

FUN FACT

In old England, it was a Sheepdog's job to guide sheep and cattle to market. The dogs' tails were docked, or "bobbed," to prove they were employed. (This way, the owner didn't have to pay a tax.) Sheepdogs are still nicknamed "Bobtails" today!

Trace your own
Old English
Sheepdog on
the transparent
paper.

ENGLISH SPRINGER SPANIEL

The lively Springer is a hunting dog with long ears, a round head, and a rectangular muzzle.

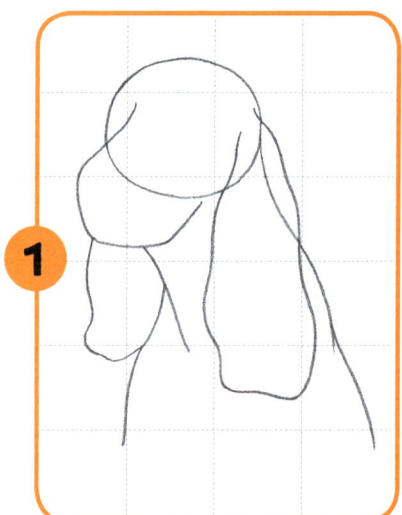
1

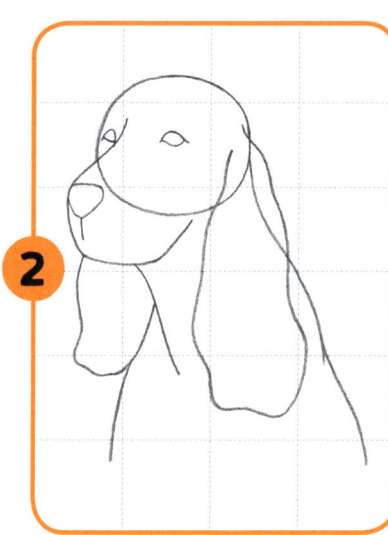
2

3

4

5

Copy the lines shown in each step. When you're done with all the steps, you'll have a complete drawing of an English Springer Spaniel. Add details to your drawing in with markers, pencils, crayons, or paints.

Step-by-Step

DACHSHUND

These low-to-the-ground pooches have long, thin bodies with a sausage shape, earning them the nickname "wiener dogs"!

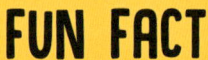

FUN FACT

The Dachshund's name comes from its first "profession"—hunting badgers! In German, "dachs" means badger and "hund" is dog. Today's Doxies are smaller in size and are used to hunt rabbits instead.

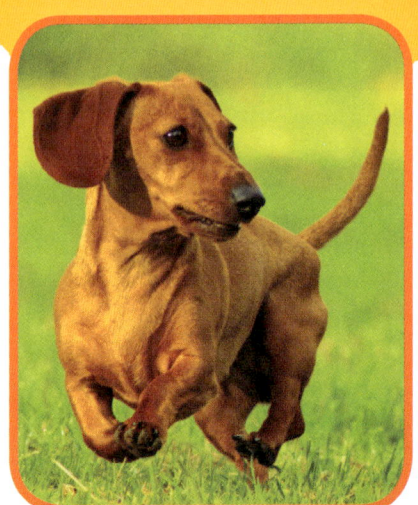

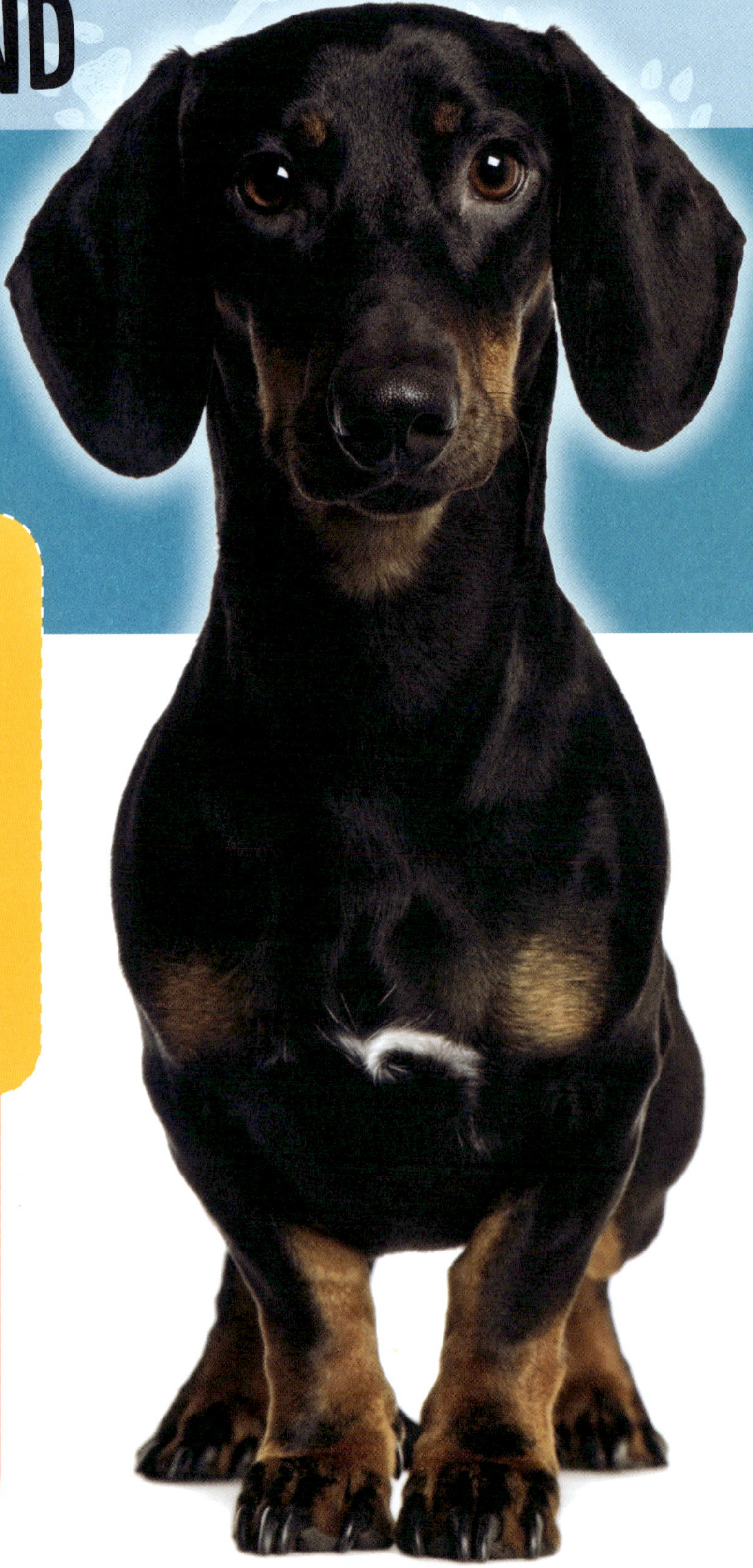

Follow along, first drawing basic shapes with light pencil lines. Copy the new lines shown in each step, eventually darkening the lines you want to keep and erasing the rest. Finally add details to your drawing with pencils, markers, paints, or crayons.

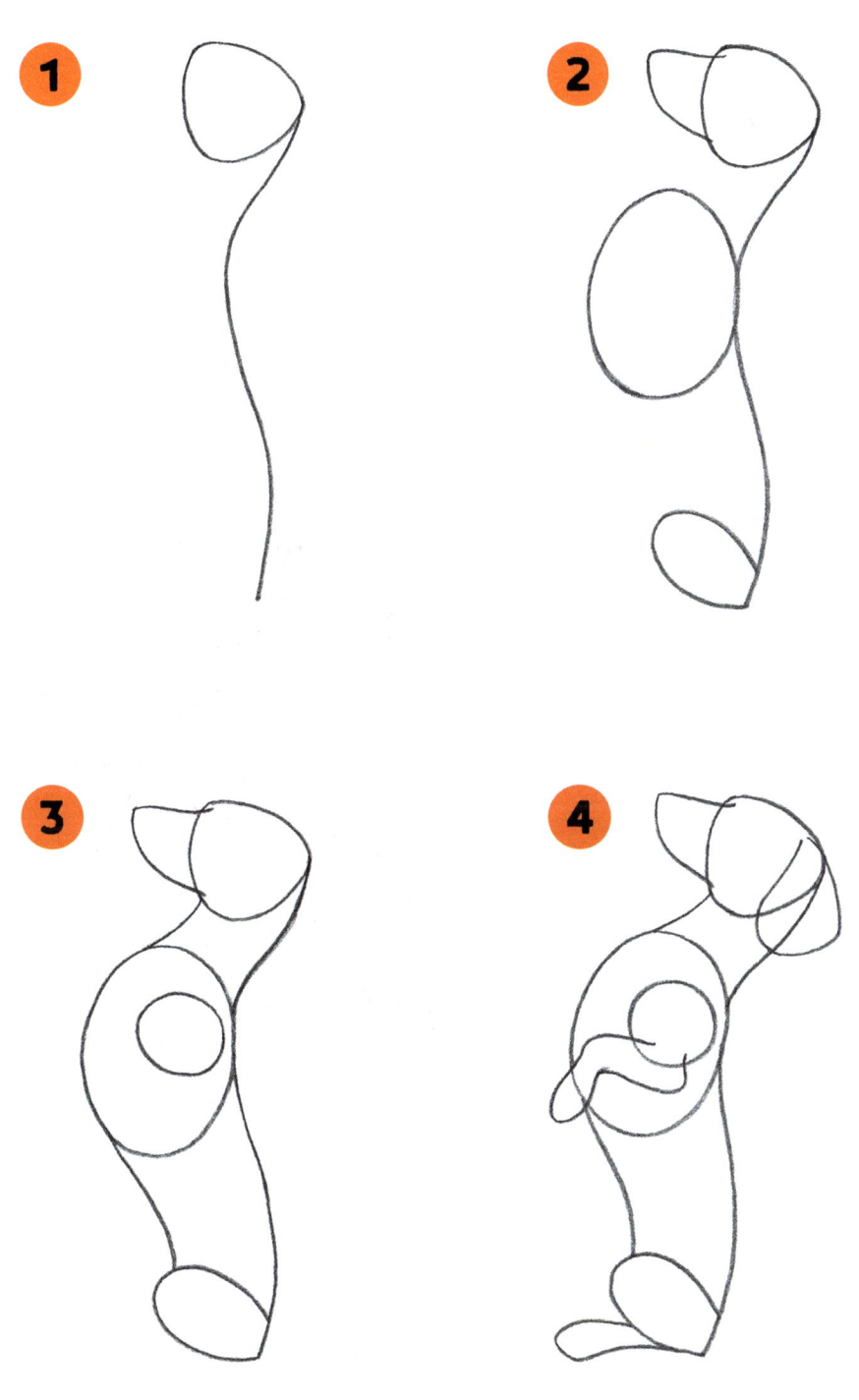

5

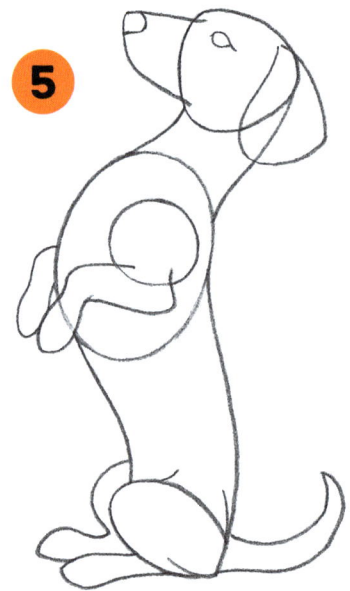

6

7

Draw your own Dachshund here!

PARSON RUSSELL TERRIER

These lovable pups are white with patches of black or tan. Their bright eyes are large and round, and their ears fold forward.

FUN FACT

This breed was named after the Reverend John ("Jack") Russell. Nicknamed "the hunting parson," the reverend developed the breed to run long distances with Foxhounds.

Trace your own Parson Russell Terrier on the transparent paper.

BOXER

Boxers are part of the working group of dog breeds; dogs in the working group are intelligent, strong, and alert, and are bred to do different jobs.

1

2

3

4

5

Copy the lines shown in each step. When you're done with all the steps, you'll have a complete drawing of a Boxer. Add details to your drawing with markers, pencils, crayons, or paints.

SIBERIAN HUSKY

The Husky is a sled dog with an athletic body, mask-like head markings, and a dense coat and bushy tail that keeps it warm.

FUN FACT

Siberian Huskies are known for their striking eyes, which range from sky blue to reddish amber. It is not uncommon for a Husky to have one blue and one amber eye (called "bi-eyed") or blue and amber in one eye (called "parti-eyed").

Follow along, first drawing basic shapes with light pencil lines. Copy the new lines shown in each step, eventually darkening the lines you want to keep and erasing the rest. Finally add details to your drawing with pencils, markers, paints, or crayons.

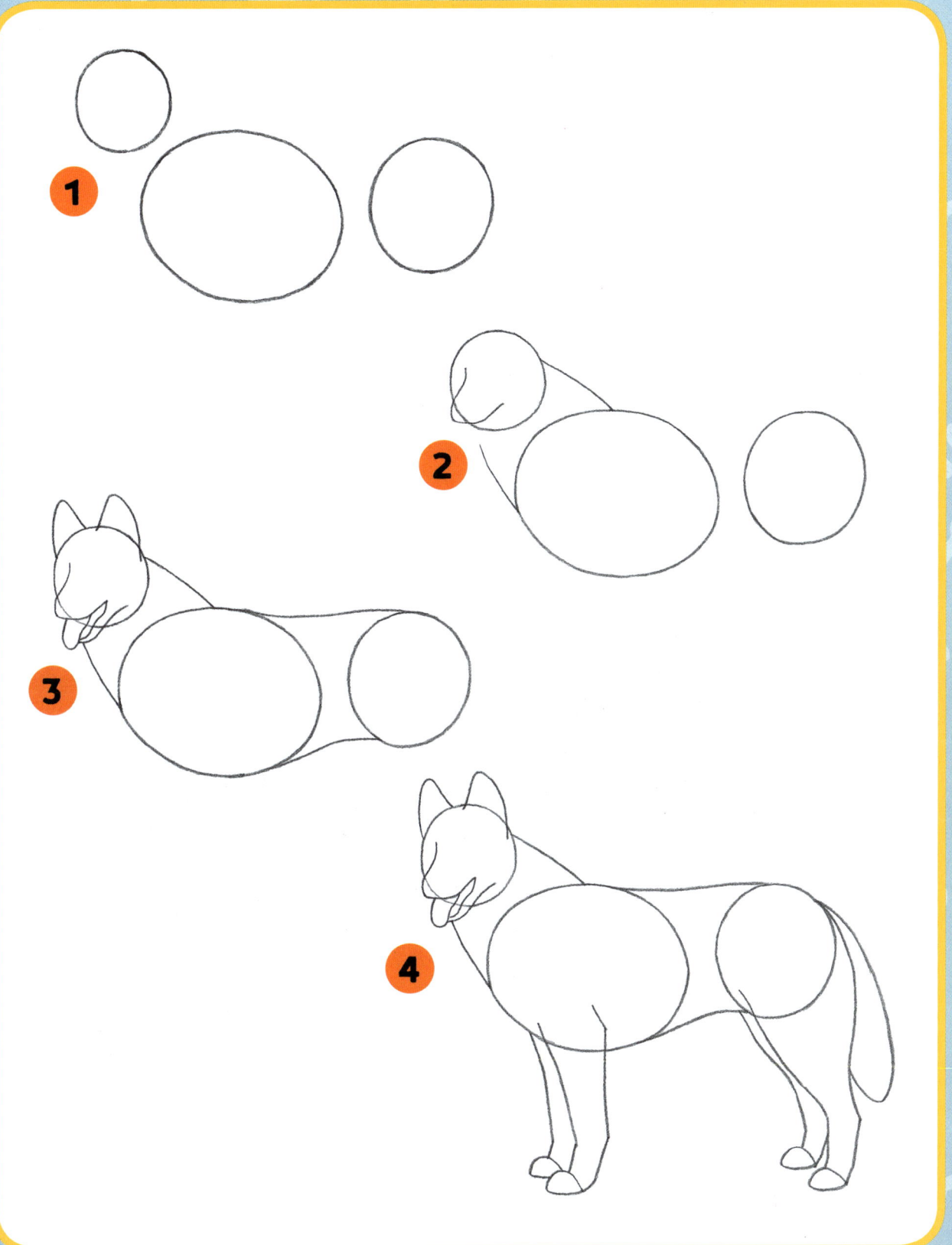

5

6

7

Draw your own Siberian Husky here!

HIDDEN HOUND

Fill in each numbered space with a matching shade from the guide below to reveal the hidden picture.

2	2	2	2	2	2	2	2	2	2	2	2	2	2	2
2	2	5	5	2	2	2	2	2	2	2	5	5	2	2
2	5	5	5	5	4	4	4	4	4	5	5	5	5	2
2	5	5	5	3	3	4	4	4	3	3	5	5	5	2
2	5	5	3	5	5	5	4	3	3	3	3	5	5	2
2	5	5	3	5	1	5	4	3	1	3	3	5	5	2
2	5	2	3	5	5	4	1	4	3	3	3	2	5	2
2	2	2	3	3	3	4	4	4	3	3	3	2	2	2
2	2	2	2	2	3	3	3	3	3	2	2	2	2	2
2	2	2	2	2	2	2	2	2	2	2	2	2	2	2

34

Answers on page 64.

PUP-POO!

There are four people, four pups, and four piles of dog poo. To clean up this mess, draw two straight lines, each one starting on one edge and running across to the other edge, to divide the park into four separate areas. These lines can be in any direction, but each area must contain exactly one person, one pup, and one poo.

Answers on page 64.

GOLDEN RETRIEVER PUPPY

Best known for their golden coats, these pups also have strong legs, round paws, and large, wide-set eyes.

FUN FACT

Since the Golden Retriever was developed in England and Scotland in the 1800s, it has had many names. Until 1920, the breed was known as the Golden Flat-Coat. They've also been called "Yellow Retrievers" and "Russian Retrievers."

Copy the lines shown in each step. When you're done with all the steps, you'll have a complete drawing of a Corgi. Add details to your drawing with markers, pencils, crayons, or paints.

GERMAN SHEPHERD

This popular breed has a long, strong body. Be sure to draw large, athletic thighs on this proud, powerful canine–and make its muzzle about half the length of its head.

FUN FACT

German Shepherds are often used as guard dogs, police dogs, and military dogs because of their athletic nature, intelligence, and obedience.

Follow along, first drawing basic shapes with light pencil lines. Copy the new lines shown in each step, eventually darkening the lines you want to keep and erasing the rest. Finally add details to your drawing with pencils, markers, paints, or crayons.

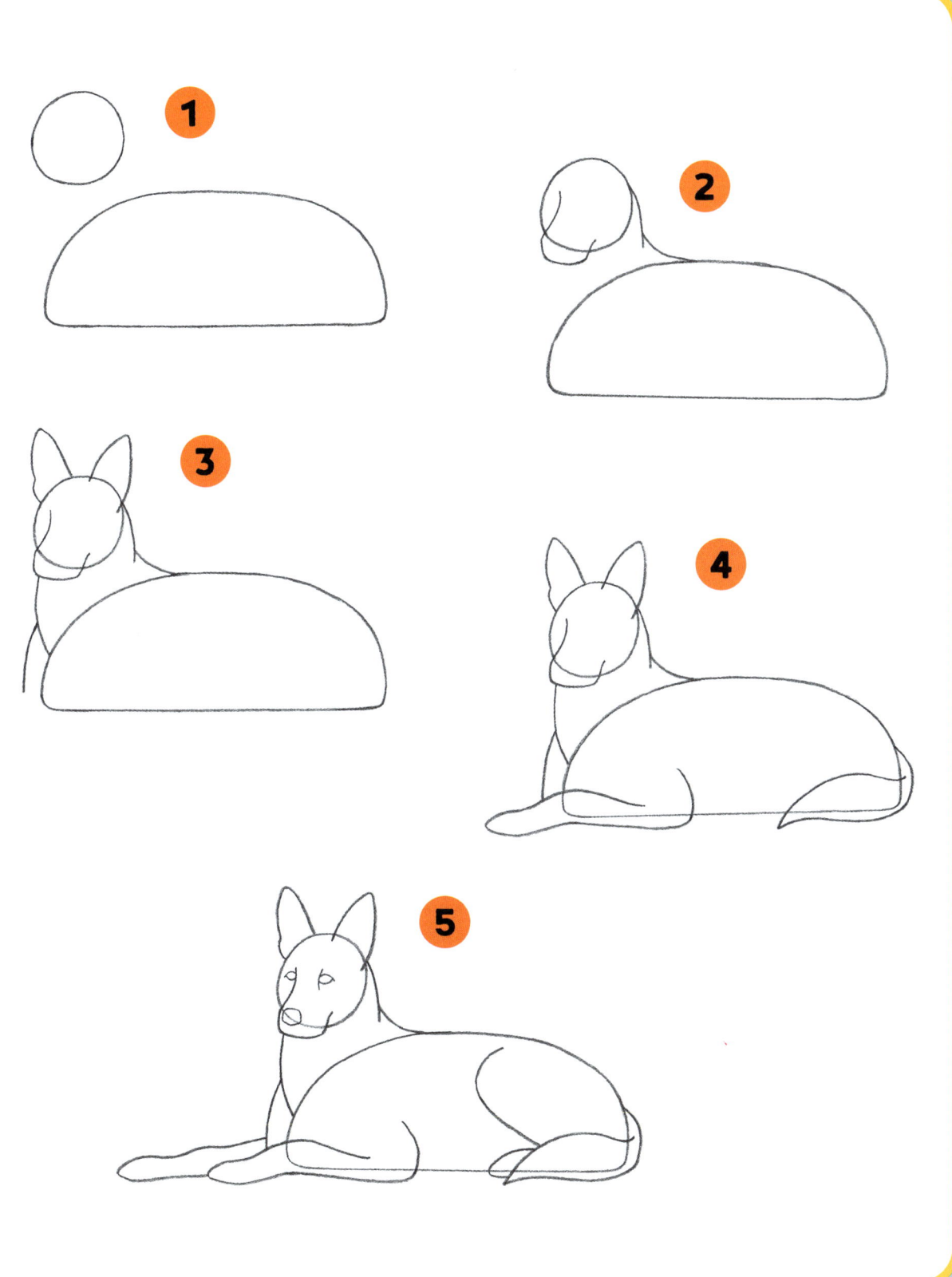

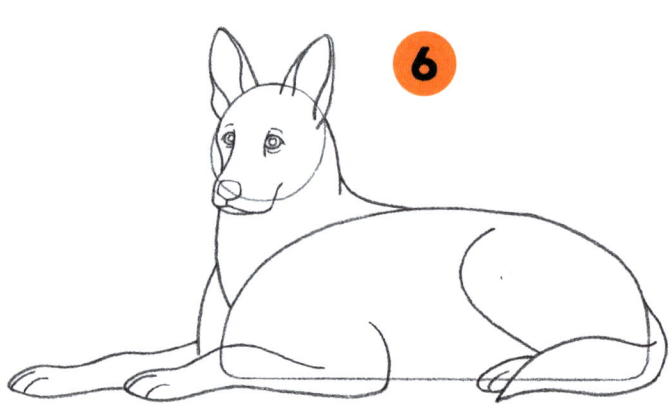

MIX-UP

Can you unscramble these dog breeds?

ODPEOL

_____

NEHDGOYUR

_____

HISH ZUT

_____

LOIECL

_____

Answers on page 64.

TAIL-WAGGING TRIVIA

1. True or False?
Dalmatians are born pure white, without spots.

2. Which breed was the first Olympic mascot?
A. Scottish Terrier
B. Chihuahua
C. Corgi

3. True or False?
Akitas were originally bred as hunting dogs in Japan.

4. True or False?
Poodles do not shed any hair.

5. Which dog breed is known for its black tongue?
A. Poodle
B. Chow Chow
C. Boxer

Answers on page 64.

DALMATIAN

Dalmatians are intelligent dogs with speed, stamina, and impressive memories.

FUN FACT

Once known for escorting horse-drawn carriages in the 18th century, including fire engines, the Dalmatian earned the nickname "Fire House Dog."

Follow along, first drawing basic shapes with light pencil lines. Copy the new lines shown in each step, eventually darkening the lines you want to keep and erasing the rest. Finally add details to your drawing with pencils, markers, paints, or crayons.

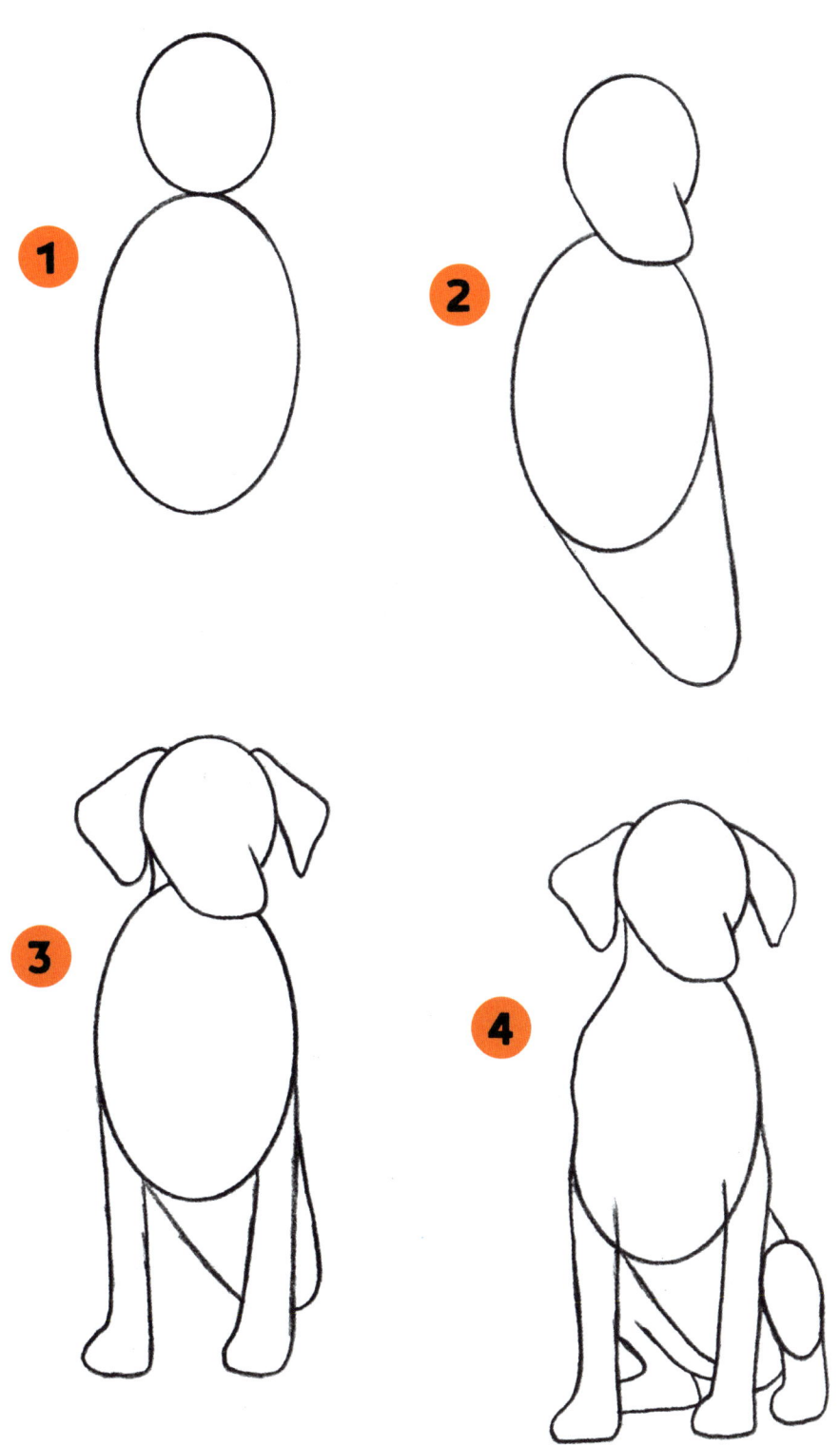

Tracing Method

GREAT DANE

Great Danes are very tall with long bodies. These loyal companions are also gentle and loving.

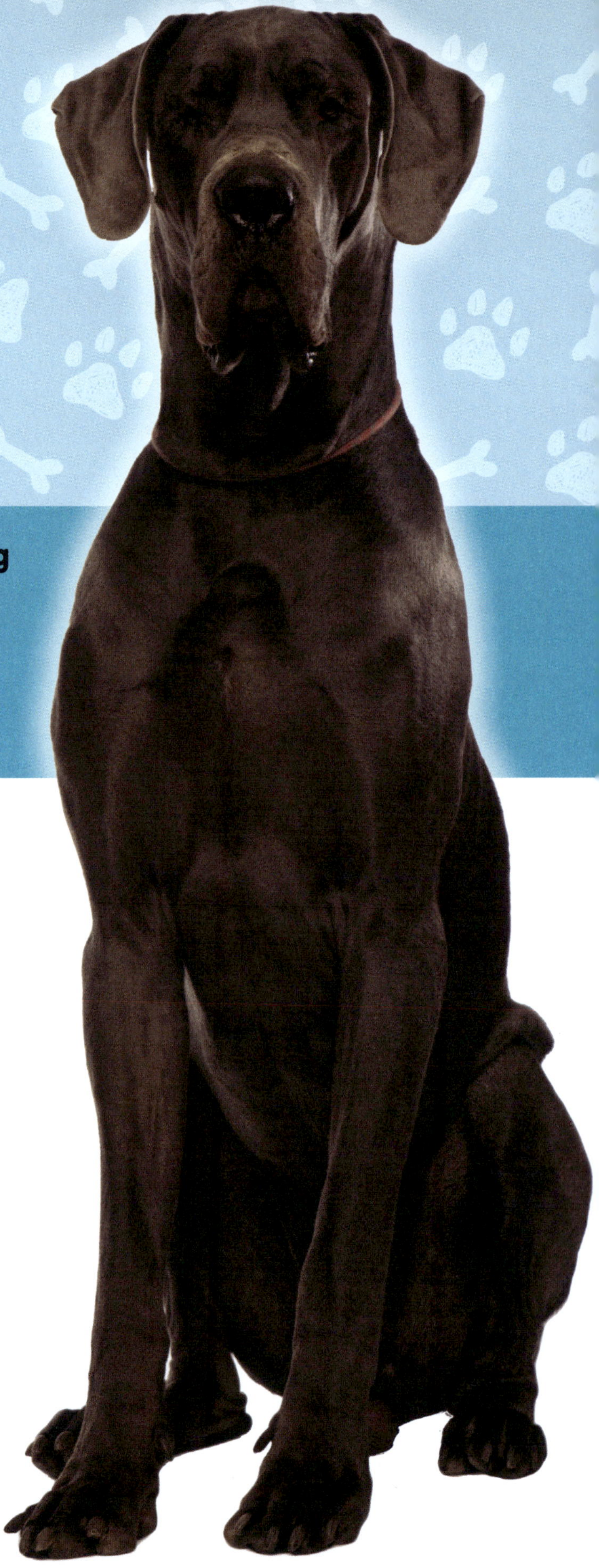

FUN FACT

The name "Great Dane" makes people think these dogs are Danish (from Denmark). But the Great Dane (also known as *Deutsche Dogge*, meaning "German Dog") is the national dog of Germany, where the breed originated.

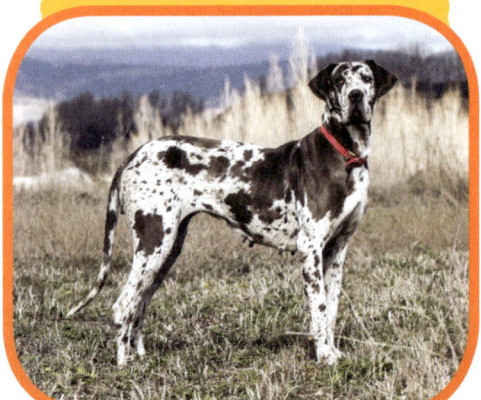

Trace your own
Great Dane on
the transparent
paper.

Step-by-Step

BULLDOG

Bulldogs have a stocky build, large head, and folded ears. Their unique faces feature a flat muzzle and an endearing overbite.

FUN FACT

Originally bred to fight bulls hundreds of years ago in Europe, these brave dogs are also called "English Bulldogs."

Follow along, first drawing basic shapes with light pencil lines. Copy the new lines shown in each step, eventually darkening the lines you want to keep and erasing the rest. Finally add details to your drawing with pencils, markers, paints, or crayons.

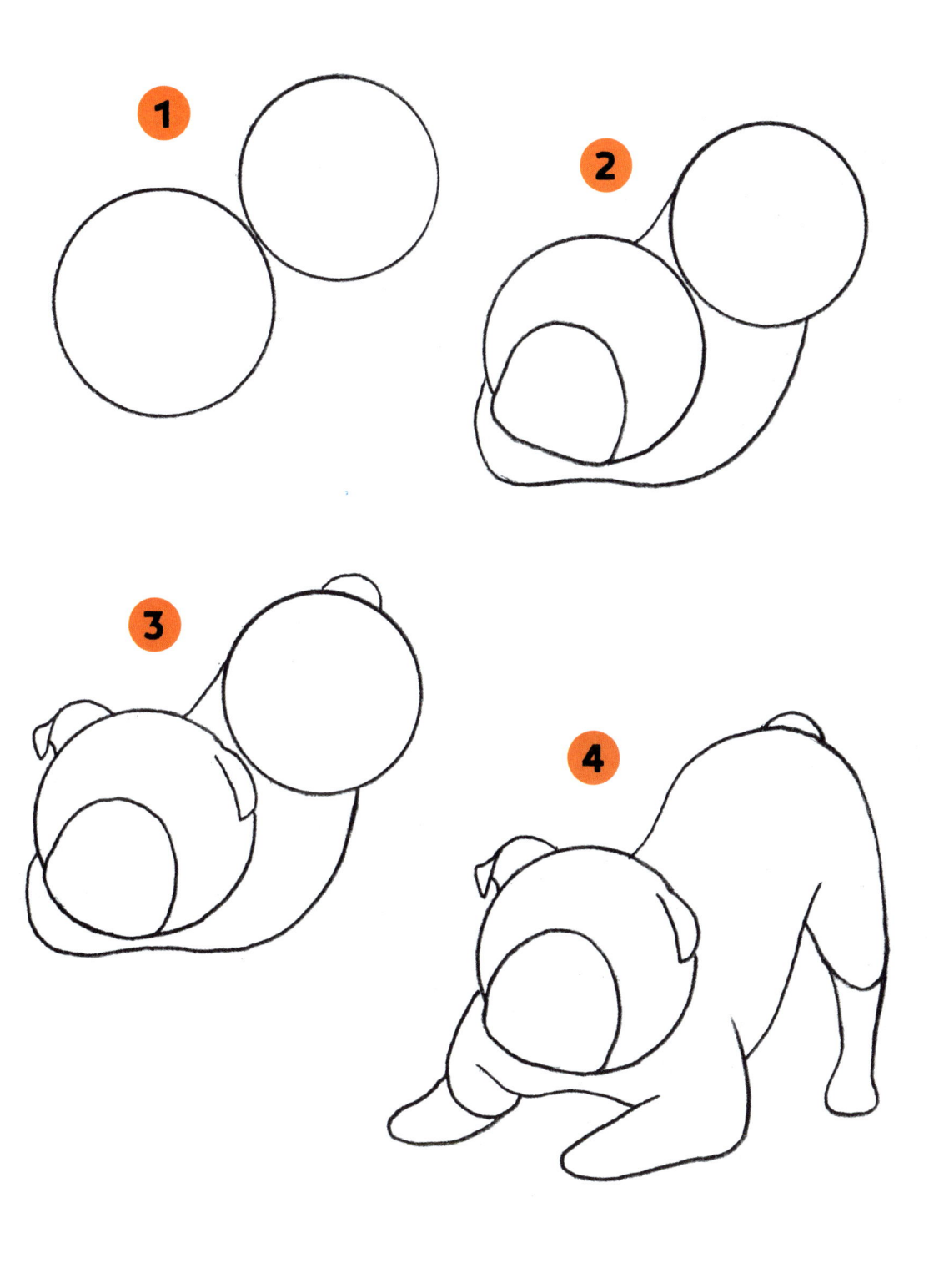

5

6

7

ALL GROWN UP!

What will these puppies look like when they grow up?
Draw a line to connect the matching breeds.

Answers on page 64.

SU-DOG-KU

Solve the sudoku puzzle by filling in the blanks using the numbers 1-9. Each number can only be used one time in a row, column, and box.

2	7		5		9	1		
	3						8	
9		6				3		2
	8			5			9	
1			6		7			
	2		1			7		8
4				6			3	
	9		3	2				6
	1				8		7	

Answers on page 64.

57

YORKSHIRE TERRIER

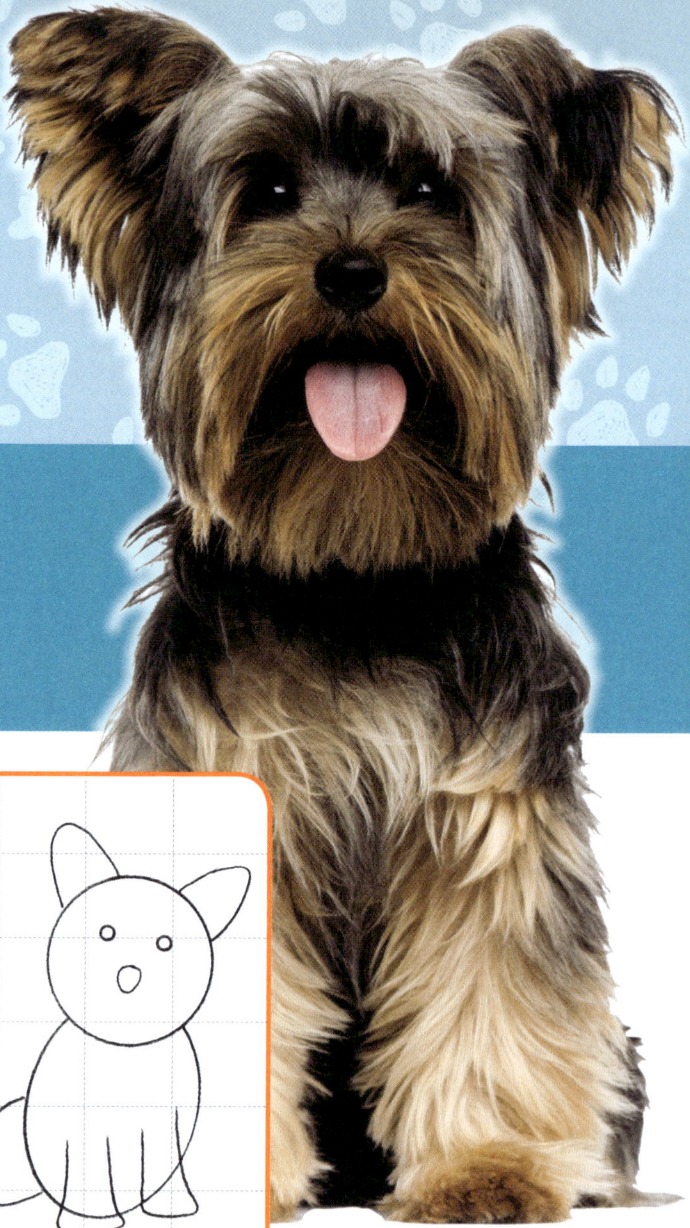

Called "Yorkies" for short, these dogs are known for their long, silky hair.

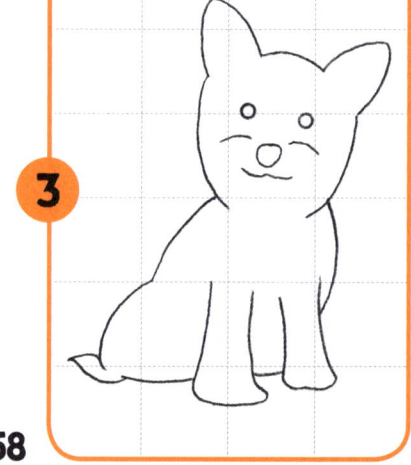

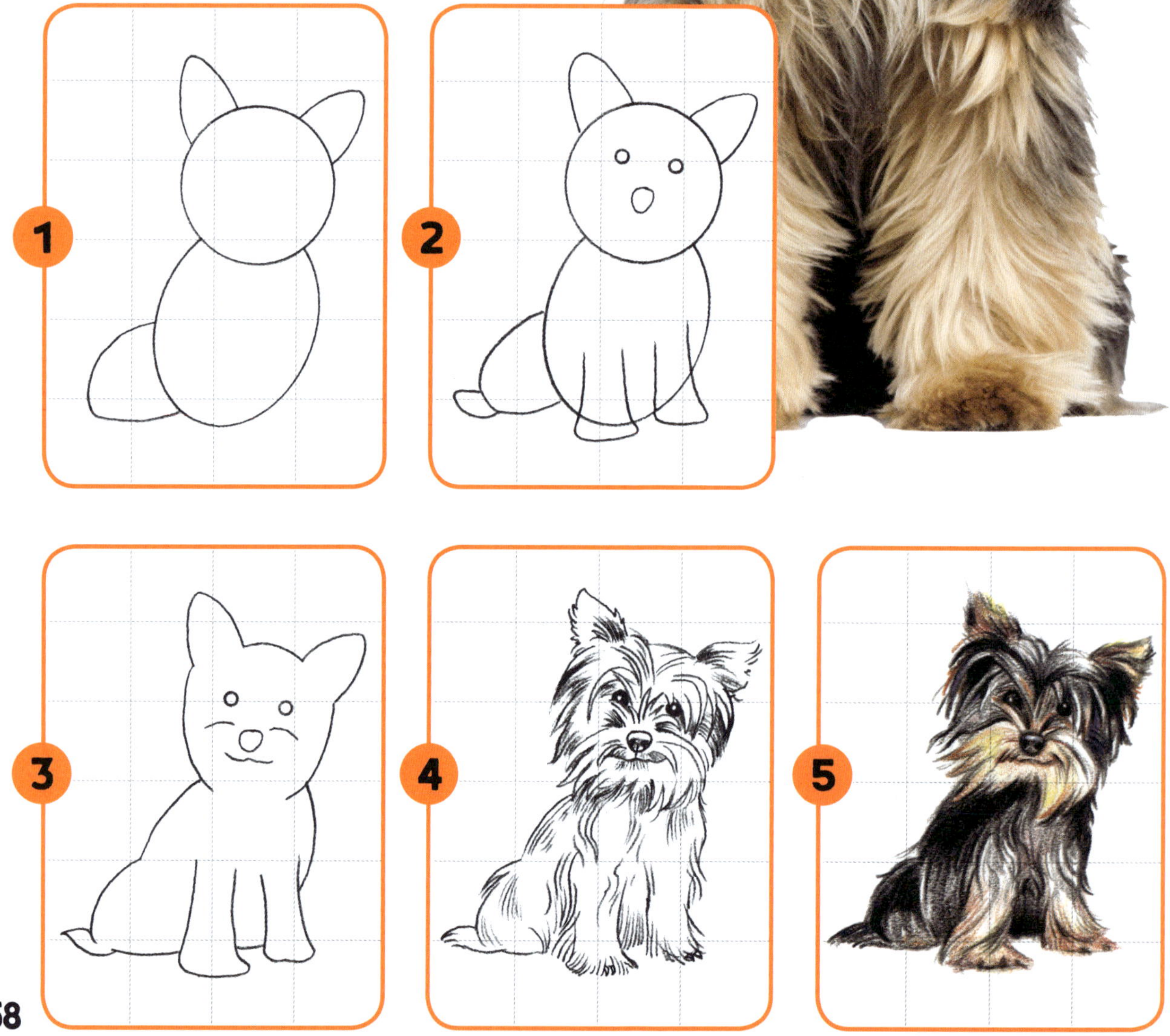

1

2

3

4

5

Copy the lines shown in each step. When you're done with all the steps, you'll have a complete drawing of a Yorkshire Terrier. Add details to your drawing with markers, pencils, crayons, or paints.

Step-by-Step

BEAGLE

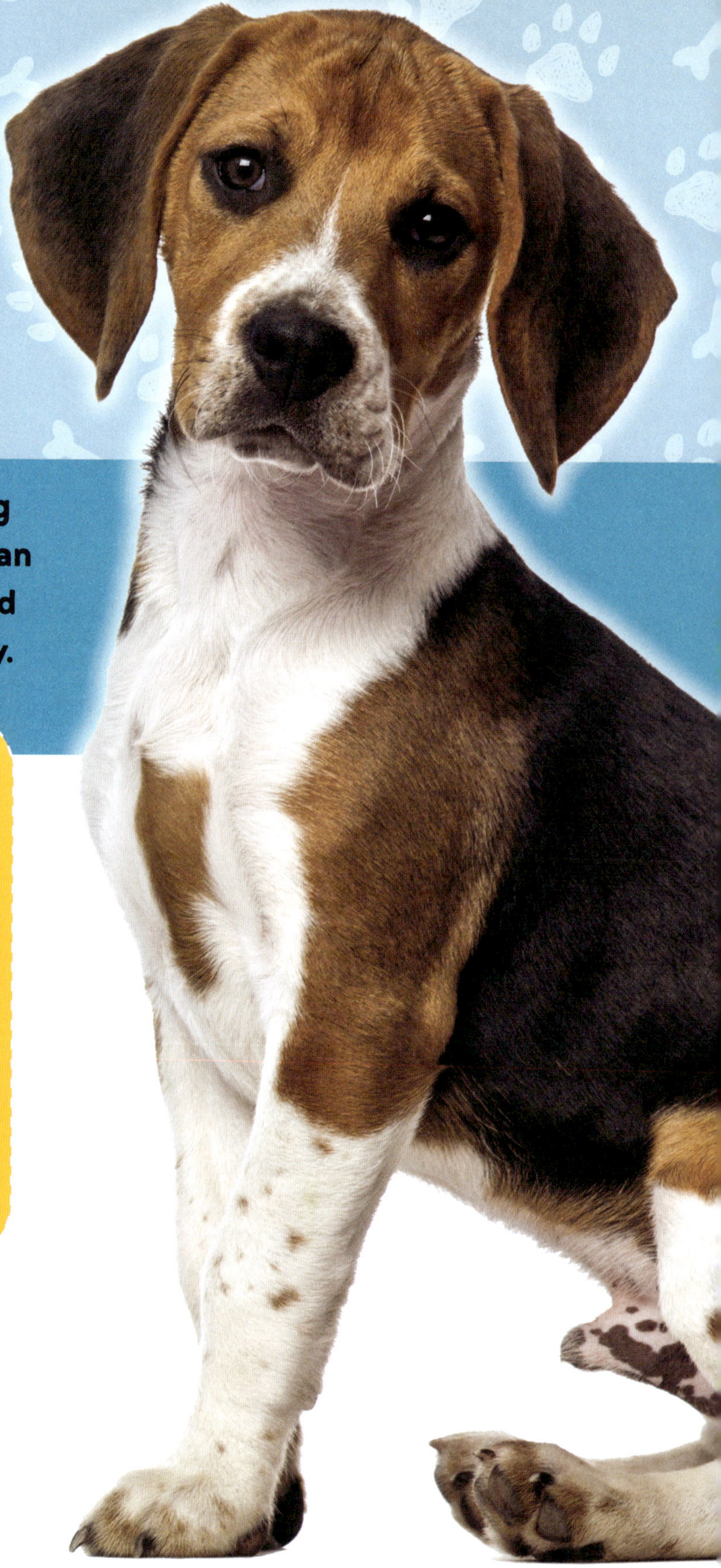

Originally bred as hunting companions, Beagles have an amazing sense of smell and remarkable howling ability.

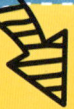

FUN FACT

This compact hound has a cheerful, energetic personality that makes it a popular family pet. But be careful! Beagles are determined escape artists; they will do whatever it takes to follow a scent—even if it leads them out of the backyard!

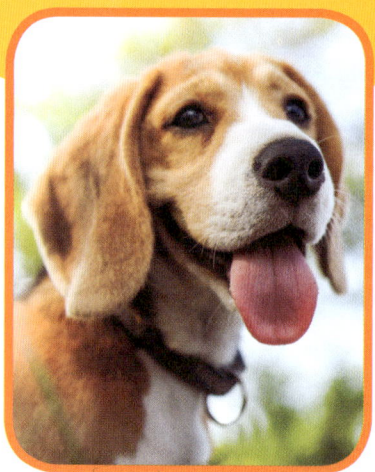

Follow along, first drawing basic shapes with light pencil lines. Copy the new lines shown in each step, eventually darkening the lines you want to keep and erasing the rest. Finally add details to your drawing with pencils, markers, paints, or crayons.

5

6

7

Draw your own Beagle here!

ANSWERS

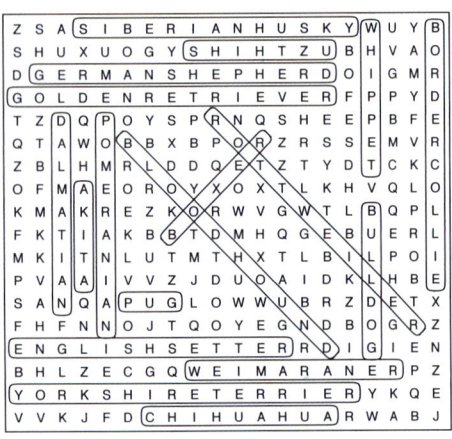

Page 16:
Dog Breed Word Search

Page 17:
Dinner Time!

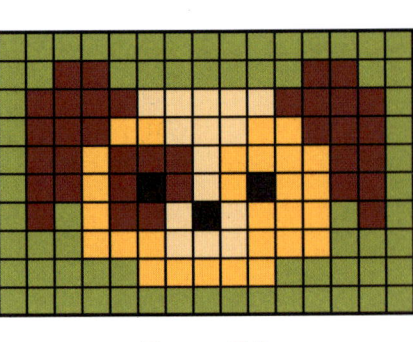

Page 34:
Hidden Hound

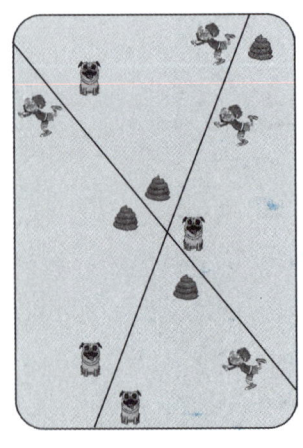

Page 35:
Pup-Poo!

POODLE

GREYHOUND

SHIH TZU

COLLIE

Page 44:
Mix-Up

1. True

2. A

3. True

4. True

5. B

Page 45:
Tail-Wagging Trivia

Page 56:
All Grown Up!

2	7	8	5	3	9	1	6	4
5	3	4	2	1	6	9	8	7
9	1	6	8	7	4	3	5	2
7	8	3	4	5	2	6	9	1
1	4	9	6	8	7	5	2	3
6	2	5	1	9	3	7	4	8
4	5	2	7	6	1	8	3	9
8	9	7	3	2	5	4	1	6
3	6	1	9	4	8	2	7	5

Page 57:
Su-Dog-Ku

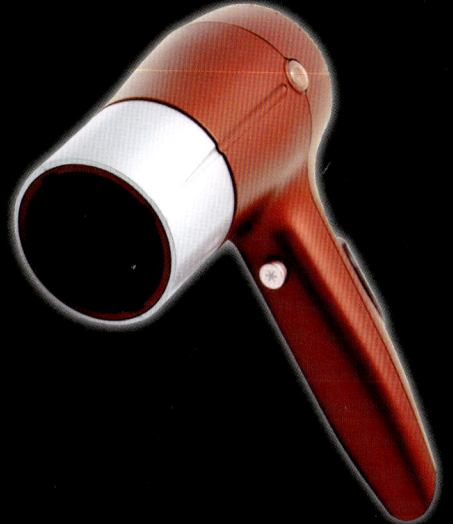

Haircare

Salon secrets of the professionals

Alexandra Friend & Sheridan Ward

A & C Black

First published in 2010 by
A&C Black Publishers
36 Soho Square
London W1D 3QY
www.acblack.com

ISBN: 978-1-4081-2994-4

This book was conceived, designed and produced by
Quintet Publishing Limited
6 Blundell Street
London N7 9BH
UK

QTT.HDB

Project Editor: Martha Burley
Editorial Assistant: Holly Willsher
Photographer: Tom & Ollie Photography
Stylist: Sheridan Ward
Makeup Artists: Denny Richards, Kenny Leung
Designer: Anna Plucinska
Illustrator: Bernard Chau
Art Director: Michael Charles
Managing Editor: Donna Gregory
Publisher: James Tavendale

This book is produced using paper that is made for wood grown in managed, sustainable forests. It is natural, renewable and recyclable. The logging and manufacturing
processes conform to the environmental regulations of the country of origin.

CONTENTS

INTRODUCTION

Tucked out of sight or worn proudly on display, hair (or sometimes even the lack of it) has been used through history to signify strength, virtue, grief and religious devotion – and still speaks volumes about us. Whether hurriedly bundled up or elaborately groomed, our hair tells the outside world about our inner selves, and always has the power to make or break our day.

A cut that goes wrong or a style that falls flat can feel like the end of the world – while hair that eases happily into position leaves us feeling on top of it. The emotional connection we have with our hair is also evident in the relationships we have with those we allow to touch it – the stylist with whom we find ourselves sharing our deepest secrets, or the friend who smooths back our unruly locks when we're upset.

So it's no wonder that we've been styling our hair since early civilisation – the Egyptians used henna to achieve vibrant hues, while the Romans used gold dust, crushed berries and vinegar. Primitive humans showed rank by accessorising with feathers and bone, while the ancient Greeks wore flowers and jewels. Hair can have social or political significance too – the shingled crops of the 1920s came hand in hand with greater freedom for women, while the wearing of natural Afros of the 1960s and '70s was associated with the black empowerment movement.

Today, we curl, straighten, colour and cut our hair to follow fashion, suit our lifestyles or complement our bone structure. We create elaborate updos for special occasions, get a short, sharp crop after a break-up, and preface some of the most important events of our lives, from first dates to job interviews, with a blow-dry.

While it can't guarantee you a promotion, this book can increase your quota of good hair days by boosting your styling know-how and demystifying the tricks of the trade. From tweaking your nutrition to tackling a salon visit, and creating looks from the simplest ponytail to the most elaborate plait, you'll find everything you need in the following pages.

ABOUT THIS BOOK

No matter how much you already know about hair, and whether you're planning to read this book from cover to cover or just dip in and out, we hope you'll discover something new and interesting every time you pick it up. Its aim is not just to teach you how to create a wide range of professional styles, but also to help you understand exactly how they're put together, so you can continue to experiment long after you've finished the last page.

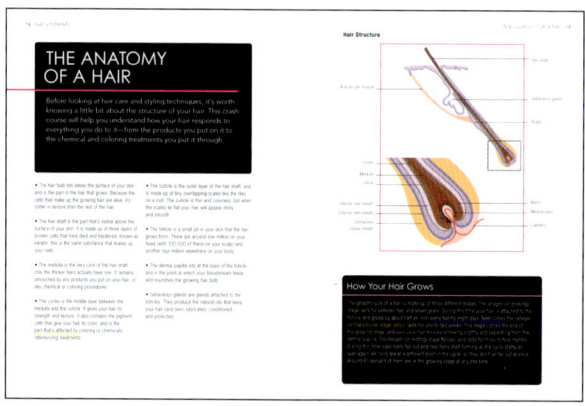

⬅ ⬆ **Chapters 1 and 2 – Raw Materials and Getting Started** – cover things you should know before you even pick up a brush! They'll help you to understand your individual hair type, how your diet, lifestyle and environment can all contribute to a good or bad hair day, and which styling tools you'll need to create the different looks in the book.

Chapters 3 and 4 – Essential Techniques and Basic Styles – will talk you through some basic skills, from washing and drying your hair to perfecting simple styles such as plaits and ponytails. As well as enhancing your everyday hair-care routine, these pages are the building blocks that will help you create the more complicated looks in the next chapter – Occasion Looks – and are worth taking some time over. As with every section of the book, each technique is broken down into bite-sized steps and accompanied with expert tips and tricks, so you'll pick up plenty of industry know-how along the way.

After the elaborate styles in **Occasion Looks**, you'll find some chapters that will extend your hair-care knowledge even further, whether it's getting more out of a visit to the salon, colouring your hair at home or trimming your fringe. Finally, a troubleshooting guide will help you tackle minor hair health issues, and shed light on why you might be finding some styles harder to achieve than others.

But before you get started, it's important to remember that practice makes perfect, and should always be fun. It's only by getting stuck that you'll find out what works and what doesn't. If something doesn't work straight away, take a break, then have another go, and you'll find that it will suddenly fall into place. We hope this book will give you the knowledge and confidence to try new things and develop your own personal techniques – the rest is up to you. Happy styling!

INTRODUCTION TO YOUR STYLIST

Sheridan Ward, co-author and hair stylist, gives us an insight into his career – and how a book like this can help everyone, whether you are interested in hair care in general, are looking to pick up a few tricks of the trade, or you want to become stylist to the stars.

About This Book

This book is a brilliant way of learning how to use simple and easy techniques – not just in caring for your hair but also creating beautiful styles at home. The book is comprised of contemporary and classic styles, but all have a modern twist. Using the step-by-step guides, and with a bit of practice, you can have wonderful hair every day and for any occasion. All the styles in this book can be crossed over and combined to create individual styles. You can add your own twist on things. When you look good, you feel good – and in life you are the most important person, so treat yourself and look fabulous every day.

The Catwalk Lifestyle

Working as a catwalk stylist can be a hectic and exciting lifestyle where you don't know where you are from one day to the next and you're always in different locations. I've had an amazing time working in Asia and all over Europe, meeting lots of fascinating people, including other creative types, famous designers, models and the odd celebrity here and there. It is vital to be prepared mentally and physically, which can be as simple as staying hydrated during a shoot or making sure you have everything you need by packing your kit bag the night before a big job. It is also vital to get to bed as early as possible and always eat breakfast. Spending hours on your feet in badly lit studios or freezing on a hilltop can be tough, but it's worth it. I have a bottle of water, vitamin C tablets, hand lotion, tissues and flu medicine with me at all times.

Career Path

I've always been creative and full of energy and I'd been cutting hair for about three years before I decided to take the plunge and study for a qualification. It started as more of a hobby; I used to watch the way they cut my hair in the salon and then I'd go home and practise the techniques I'd seen on my little sister. Once I had qualified, I worked in a few salons before deciding to go out on my own. I organised my own shoot, paid a photographer and got a couple of friends to model for me. Once I got the pictures back I started to build my own portfolio. I found a few networking sites on the internet where I had the chance to network with other creative types, such as photographers and makeup artists. I started doing test shoots (working for free with different creative people to produce beautiful images). I continued building my portfolio, then started to approach hair and makeup agencies and was lucky enough to land a place on shows during London Fashion Week – the rest is history.

Pro Tips for a Career in Styling

- Take a course.
- Network with people who are in the industry.
- Assist a professional and see if it's for you.
- Speak to your hairstylist – ask what they like about it and how they got into it.
- Think about the area you would like to specialise in. Career choices in hair care include: working in or owning a salon; wedding or special occasions hair; working for private clients; working on fashion shows and magazine photo shoots; and working in film and TV.

Chapter **1**

RAW MATERIALS

Getting the most out of your hair means knowing it from the inside out. From identifying your hair type to tweaking your diet, this chapter will help you get yours into the best possible condition before you even pick up a brush.

THE ANATOMY OF A HAIR

Before looking at hair care and styling techniques, it's worth knowing a little bit about the structure of your hair. This crash course will help you understand how your hair responds to everything you do to it – from the products you put on it to the chemical and colouring treatments you put it through.

- The hair bulb sits below the surface of your skin and is the part of the hair that grows. Because the cells that make up the growing hair are alive, it's softer in texture than the rest of the hair.

- The hair shaft is the part that's visible above the surface of your skin. It is made up of three layers of protein cells that have died and hardened. Known as keratin, this is the same substance that makes up your nails.

- The medulla is the very core of the hair shaft; only the thicker hairs actually have one. It remains untouched by any products you put on your hair, or any chemical or colouring procedures.

- The cortex is the middle layer between the medulla and the cuticle. It gives your hair its strength and texture. It also contains the pigment cells that give your hair its colour, and is the part that's affected by colouring or chemically retexturising treatments.

- The cuticle is the outer layer of the hair shaft, and is made up of tiny overlapping scales like the tiles on a roof. The cuticle is thin and colourless, but when the scales lie flat your hair will appear shiny and smooth.

- The follicle is a small pit in your skin that the hair grows from. There are around one million on your head (with 100,000 of these on your scalp) and another four million elsewhere on your body.

- The dermal papilla sits at the base of the follicle, and is the point at which your bloodstream feeds and nourishes the growing hair bulb.

- Sebaceous glands are glands attached to the follicles. They produce the natural oils that keep your hair (and skin) lubricated, conditioned and protected.

Hair Structure

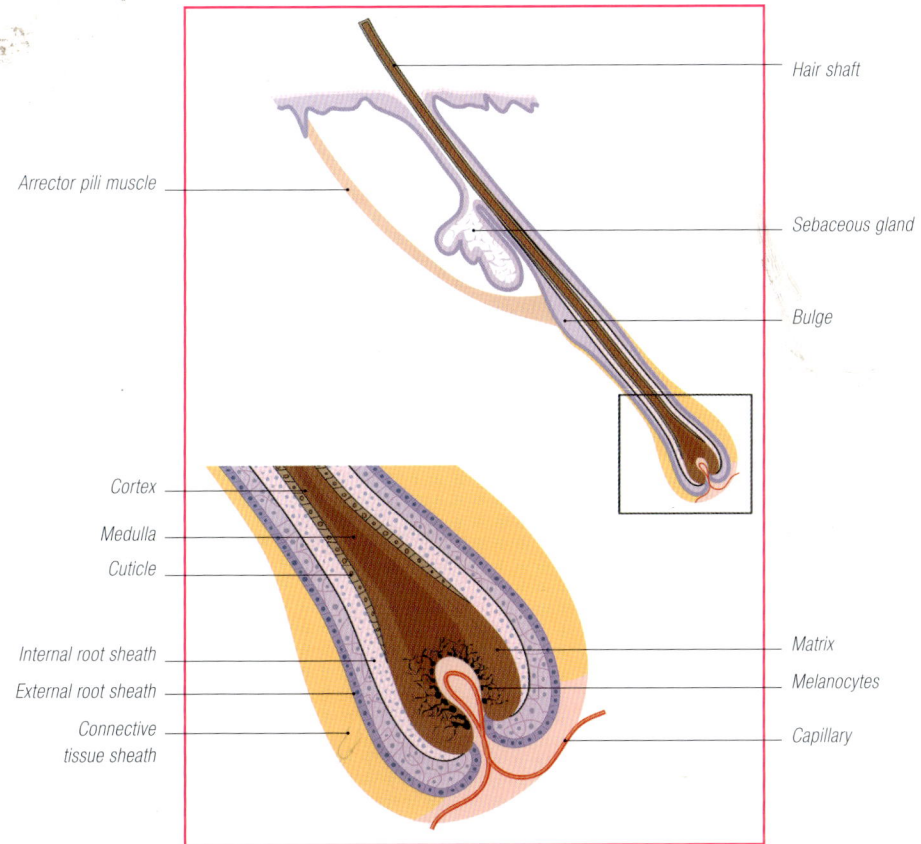

Hair shaft

Arrector pili muscle

Sebaceous gland

Bulge

Cortex

Medulla

Cuticle

Internal root sheath

External root sheath

Connective
tissue sheath

Matrix

Melanocytes

Capillary

How Your Hair Grows

The growth cycle of a hair is made up of three different stages. The anagen (or growing) stage lasts for between two and seven years. During this time your hair is attached to the follicle and grows by about a centimetre every twenty-eight days. Next comes the categen (or transitional) stage, which lasts for one to two weeks. This stage signals the end of the growing stage, and sees your hair follicles shrinking slightly and separating from the dermal papilla. The telogen (or resting) stage follows, and lasts for three to four months. During this time older hairs fall out and new hairs start forming as the cycle starts all over again. All hairs are at a different point in the cycle, so they don't all fall out at once. Around 85 per cent of them are in the growing stage at any one time.

YOUR HAIR TYPE

The first step in finding a style to suit you is to understand *your* hair type. Deciphering a few key terms and knowing how they relate to your hair will not only help you choose the right styling products, but also to work out why your hair behaves as it does, and why some styles, cuts and colouring techniques will work better than others.

Fine, Medium or Coarse?

This refers to the diameter of each individual strand. Naturally blonde hair is usually the narrowest (or finest) of all, while the darker and curlier your hair, the wider (or coarser) it tends to be.

• Fine hair usually looks softer, shinier and silkier than coarser types, but can also look flatter and is more fragile. Mousses, thickening sprays and heated styling tools create volume, while highlights or lowlights can give an illusion of fullness and depth. Shorter styles of one length (bobs, for example) usually look the fullest, unless you have lots of hair, in which case a few layers will add volume.

• Medium hair is the most versatile type of all. Not too fine and not too coarse, it's easy to manage, has plenty of movement, responds well to straightening and curling techniques, and holds styles and volume for longer than fine hair.

• Coarse hair feels rougher and heavier and can be harder to control, although it's usually stronger and more resilient, and will look thick and healthy with the right cut. Wearing it longer than chin length can control the volume by weighing it down, while layers can lighten it up – or choose short cuts that like lots of texture.

Thick or Thin?

Whether your hair is thick or thin refers to density –
or how much hair you have on your head. The
average head of hair is made up of between
100,000 and 150,000 strands. The closer you
are to the full 150,000, the thicker your hair,
while particularly thin hair may have around
90,000 strands.

• Thin hair can be plumped up with chemical
colouring or texturising treatments (but be wary
of damage if hair is fine as well as thin). A fringe or
a zigzag parting can make thin hair seem thicker,
as can volumising hair care, but avoid weighing
hair down with too much styling product. If you
use masks or treatments, look for strengthening
protein packs rather than oil-based, deep-
conditioning formulations.
• Thick hair can be hard to control, especially if it's
medium or coarse in diameter too. Whether you
choose layers or a blunt cut, it must always be well
structured and regularly trimmed, to minimise bulk
and define its shape.

Curly or Straight?

If you could cut a hair in half and look at the cross
section through a microscope, you'd see how the
shape of its shaft relates to its texture.

• Straight hair has a round shaft. It tends to shine
more than curlier types because sebum can travel
from root to tip with greater ease. The best cuts for
straight hair are blunt cuts, but avoid too much
layering as straight hair is often fine.
• Curly or wavy hair has an oval or elliptical shaft.
Because the sebum can't travel as easily from
roots to ends, it can look drier and duller than
straight hair.
• Asian hair tends to have a rounder shaft than
Caucasian hair, so is usually straighter.
• Afro-Caribbean hair is even flatter (almost
ribbon-like) and alternates from thick to thin all the
way down the shaft. This means it can break easily
at the thinnest points, so is more fragile and
less elastic.

How to Identify Your Hair Type

If you regularly blow-dry or straighten your hair, or use a styling product every day, it may have been a while since you really looked at your natural texture. Allowing your hair to dry naturally will show you what it looks like when left to its own devices – and will help you care for it accordingly.

step 1

Wash your hair with a shampoo designed for a 'normal' hair type, but don't use conditioner.

step 2

After blotting gently, allow your hair to dry naturally, without using a dryer or towelling too roughly.

step 3

Once your hair is dry, look at your natural texture. Is your hair totally straight or is there a slight kink? If your hair has waves, how many are there and are they loose or defined, regular or random? If you have curls, are they loose or tight, spirals, S-shaped or zigzag, or bouncy or stiff? Perhaps you have a mixture of textures? If so, what's the overall effect?

The natural texture of the top image is straight, silky and fine. The hair texture of the bottom image seems porous, with a natural curl.

step 4

Has frizz formed, or does your hair seem fluffy? Does it have a natural shine, look dry and dull, or is it a mixture of the two? Do the ends seem split and frayed?

step 5

To measure the thickness and texture of your individual strands, pull out a single hair and look at it in front of a piece of white paper. If the hair is barely visible and feels soft, it is fine. If it's easy to see but still feels soft, your hair is medium. If it looks thick and feels wiry, your hair is coarse.

How Porous is Your Hair?

• When hair is porous, it means it's easier for moisture to penetrate through the cuticles into its inner structure. The more porous your hair, the more styling product it will soak up, and the more time it may take to dry after washing. Porous hair also absorbs more moisture from the air, so will frizz up when the weather is humid.
• Hair that's been coloured or chemically treated is often more porous than 'virgin' hair. This is because the cuticles have been damaged and the surface of the hair isn't watertight.
• The best way to tackle porosity is by using deep-conditioning treatments that flatten the cuticle and styling products that coat the outside of the hair shaft to keep out unwanted moisture and stop frizz from forming.

Pro Tip

Noting how long your hair takes to dry naturally is another way of measuring its thickness and texture. Thin, fine hair usually dries in under an hour, whereas thick or coarse hair takes an hour or more to dry.

step 6

To measure the thickness of your hair, pull it back as if you were creating a ponytail, and measure the circumference of the tail (you can get a rough idea by seeing where your finger and thumb meet). If the circumference of the tail is five centimetres or less, you have fine hair. If it's between five and ten centimetres, your hair is of medium thickness. If the circumference measures more than ten centimetres, you have thick hair.

ENVIRONMENT AND LIFESTYLE

The world around you can affect the way your hair looks and feels... and that includes your lifestyle, environment and day-to-day routine. You will be unable to change many of these factors, but understanding why your hair behaves as it does can help you introduce some preventative measures.

What the Weather Does

In dry conditions hair can feel dry, look flat and be more prone to static because of the lack of moisture in the air. This can apply in hot or cold climates, as well as in centrally heated environments. Try deep-conditioning treatments (but keep conditioner away from the roots if your hair is limp), keep bowls of water near or on radiators to put moisture back into indoor environments, and mist on a light coat of hairspray before leaving the house. Silk-lined hats and silk pillowcases can also help to fight static.

In wet or humid conditions hair can absorb too much moisture, leaving it puffed up or weighed down, or frizzy and unmanageable – and naturally wavy or curly hair that's been straightened won't last long before reverting to type. Use deep-conditioning treatments to moisturise from the inside, choose styles that work with your natural texture, and try frizz-proof styling aids that coat your hair to create a barrier against the outside world.

What's in Your Water?

The quality of the water you use to wash your hair is another factor that can affect its condition – and can explain why your hair sometimes looks and feels different when you're away from home. Hard water has a high mineral content, which can leave hair feeling rough and make shampoo less likely to lather. Although soft water doesn't rinse away your hair-care products quite as well, it often leaves your hair softer (and sometimes flatter) than usual.

Everyday Styling Dos and Don'ts

While curling tongs, straighteners, hair dryers and styling products help you control the texture of your hair on a daily basis, overuse can leave hair dry, dull and porous.

Do...

... give your hair a break by letting it dry naturally whenever you can, and minimising alcohol-laden styling products such as mousse and hairspray.

... towel-dry your hair by gently blotting the moisture away before you start to blow-dry, so you can minimise its exposure to the hot air.

... repair the damage done by excessive use of heated tools with moisturising and conditioning masks and protein packs.

Don't ...

... let your tools get too hot, or work on the same section over and over again.

... use heated tools without applying a heat-protective styling aid to your hair first.

... overuse silicone-based styling aids (such as serum) to cover up poor condition. Silicone make hair temporarily smooth and frizz free, but overuse can leave hair limp. Instead, try something that smoothes from the outside but also contains conditioning ingredients, such as grooming cream or leave-in conditioner.

Oily, Dry or Normal?

While your hair type is unlikely to change much through your lifetime, the amount of sebum your scalp produces can vary. You'll know if yours produces too much or too little – while normal sebum production will keep your hair shiny and supple, inactive oil glands can lead to dry or brittle hair, and if your glands pump out too much oil your hair can look lank, lifeless and greasy, and will need washing more frequently. But environmental and lifestyle factors can also contribute, as can the way you care for your hair. Here are some points to watch out for…

• Hormones that are disturbed by stress levels or the birth control pill can stimulate sebum production. These factors aren't easy to tackle, but it's worth thinking about what you can change or eliminate.
• Overcleansing with harsh shampoos, overly hot water and vigorous pummelling (or even just washing too frequently) can dry out your hair and scalp, which prompts your oil glands to produce too much sebum (see the guidelines for washing your hair on page 56).

• Overbrushing can also stimulate oil production. Great if your hair is dry, not so good if it's already oily – in which case, be gentle, and avoid brushing the scalp itself.
• Poor diet can lead to a deficiency in healthy fats, leaving scalp and hair dry and dull (see the nutrition guide on page 26).

Healthy Body, Healthy Hair

As with your skin, the best building blocks are often the most basic. A body that's well fed, well rested and exercised regularly is more likely to produce strong and resilient hair. Boring yes, but also pretty foolproof.

HAIR NUTRITION

Although it takes a while for the foods you eat to affect your hair, you can improve its condition with a nutrient-packed diet. The aim is to provide the scalp and follicles with the energy they need to produce strong, healthy hair. Start by making a few tweaks to your diet, but expect to wait for anything between two and six months before you notice a difference.

While a sensible diet isn't as glamorous as a bottle of expensive supplements, it's the most sustainable way to keep your hair healthy. Providing your body with a steady supply of protein, minerals and nutrients will boost healthy cell production and keep your skin and nails well conditioned too. It's also wise to avoid crash or fad diets, as a sudden deficiency in healthy fats or vitamins and minerals can show up a few months later in the form of weak or brittle spots, or a loss of shine and vibrancy.

Hair Gets Thirsty Too

Just like your skin, hair needs to be well hydrated to stay strong and supple. Around eight to ten glasses of still water a day should keep moisture levels topped up – and don't forget that the moisture content of fresh fruit and vegetables can also contribute.

Something Extra

If you do want to take a hair-friendly supplement, try something you're less likely to find in your daily diet.

- MSM is a naturally occurring sulphur compound that boosts faster, stronger hair growth.
- Horsetail extract is rich in silica, a mineral that promotes strength, shine and softness.
- Green superfoods such as alfalfa, chlorella and blue-green algae contain amino acids for thicker, stronger hair.
- Seaweed promotes thicker and more lustrous hair as it contains a rich source of iron and calcium.

Ten Superfoods for Healthy Hair

❶ Eggs are packed with protein – and as protein forms almost 100 per cent of every hair on your head, a good supply is vital. Eggs are also rich in B vitamins, including B12 and B7 (usually known as biotin, this keeps hair supple and shiny).

❷ Oily fish is another great source of protein and also of essential fatty acids (EFAs). Your body does not produce these naturally, and without them hair can look dull and dry. The best sources of EFAs include salmon, mackerel and tuna (which is less oily but still rich in EFAs).

❸ Nuts contain healthy fats and hair-friendly minerals such as selenium (found mainly in Brazil nuts) and zinc (try almonds, cashews and walnuts).

❹ Seeds can be a good source of EFAs for non-fish eaters – particularly flax, which can be ground and sprinkled on salads or in breakfast cereals.

❺ Dark, leafy greens are rich in calcium (which promotes strong hair growth), iron (which helps to get oxygen to the follicles) and vitamins C and A (which boost circulation and regulate sebum production). Try chard, kale, spinach and broccoli.

❻ Red, orange and yellow fruits and vegetables such as mangoes, carrots, citrus fruits, sweet potatoes and tomatoes contain vitamins A and C, which help to keep your scalp healthy.

❼ Beans and pulses are a great source of protein (especially for vegetarians) and also provide iron, zinc and biotin (which helps prevent hair from becoming brittle).

❽ Whole grains found in breakfast cereals and wholegrain breads contain zinc, iron and B vitamins, and help to regulate the body's energy levels.

❾ Dairy is another great source of protein, and also contains calcium, to promote hair growth. Yoghurt and cottage cheese are an easy way to boost dairy intake without adding too much fat.

❿ Red meat and poultry are good sources of protein, iron and B vitamins.

HOLIDAY HAIR CARE

Holidays can give your hair quite a battering – but a week of sun, sand and saltwater isn't the end of the world. Although each of these things can disturb the protective cuticles on the surface of your hair (which can leave it temporarily weak and dehydrated), it's what you do to your hair while it's in this weakened state that can cause more damage than the holiday itself.

On holiday, your priorities are usually to remove chlorine deposits, salty water, sand and sunscreen from your hair without stressing it even further after a dehydrating day in the sun. Here's how...

• Shampoo should be as gentle as possible, but capable of cleansing properly. Post-swimming or after-sun formulations are designed to gently remove pool and seawater from your hair without stripping, or try moisturising versions of your usual shampoo.

• Conditioner should be as moisturising as possible. Again, try an after-sun formulation to rehydrate dried-out hair, and take a few sachets of a deep-conditioning treatment to use at the end of the day.

Hair Protection

UV light can break down the protein in your hair, leaving it dry and fragile. And while you might like the pretty sun-bleached effect you get after a few days in the sun, you'll soon lose shine and flexibility, and dark hair can look faded, dull and lacklustre. Look for styling products with a UV filter, and apply throughout the day – lightweight or oil-free sprays are the easiest to reapply without disturbing your style. Many of these products also contain conditioning ingredients, such as vitamins, and should wash out easily at the end of the day.

Holiday Styling

- Keep long hair securely tied away if you're on a breezy beach. The combined effects of wind, sand and sea salt is a little like having your hair sandpapered, and having to brush out the tangles at the end of the day can damage it even further. Try a firm plait or bun rather than a loose ponytail.
- Wearing your hair in a bun or looped ponytail will keep the ends and tips (which are the weakest areas) safely away from the drying effects of the sun.
- Best of all is a hat or headscarf – as well as protecting your hair, this will also protect your scalp (which can burn easily) from the sun.
- Slicking your hair back with conditioner while you're on the beach or by the pool is a common holiday tip, but if your hair heats up too much, the oils in the product can 'fry' the hair. Instead of a regular conditioner or hair mask, look for a leave-in conditioner with UV protection, or an oil or balm with sunscreen ingredients.

Pro Tip

Avoid having your hair coloured just before a holiday. Following up the potentially damaging colouring process with a big dose of sun and chlorine could not only damage your hair further, but also alter the effect of the colour itself. Leave at least three weeks between colouring your hair and going on holiday, or have it done just after you get back, when your stylist can also apply a restorative treatment and trim away any damaged ends.

From Day to Night

What you do at the end of the day can make or break the health of your hair. Avoid using hair dryers, curling tongs or straighteners if possible, or at least use a thermal-protective product before you start styling. Some styling products can dehydrate your hair, so use balms and creams rather than mousse or hairspray, or look for alcohol-free versions.

Humidity

Humid conditions mean more moisture in the air, which your hair will soak up to become frizzy and fluffy, or lank and flat. The best way to protect against this is with a styling product that acts as a barrier, such as a cream or balm.

Heat-free Styling

- Try plaiting damp hair in the morning (run a protective styling cream through the lengths and ends first), let it dry throughout the day and untie in the evening for a waved effect.
- Pull damp hair back into a sleek bun or ponytail after washing in the evening, applying a serum or balm first to fight frizz.
- Work with the texturizing effect of the salt, sun and sand by scrunching a beach-effect styling spray through your hair and letting it air-dry.

Pro Tips

- Prepare your hair for a holiday by packing it full of moisture. Try applying a conditioning treatment twice a week for two or three weeks before you go.
- Rinse your hair under an outdoor shower before jumping into the pool. Hair that's already wet will soak up less chlorinated water, which can leave lighter hair looking brassy or even greenish. Rinse again when you get out of the water.

Sea salt sprays like this one from international brand GHD are a great product for working your sun-kissed tresses into a style.

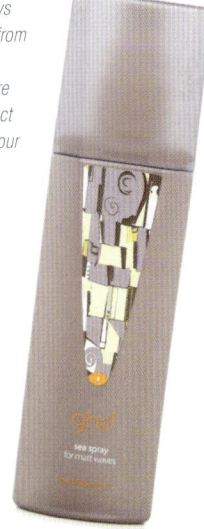

Chapter (2)

GETTING STARTED

Whether it's a set of sectioning clips or a final mist of shine spray, this chapter explains how to choose (and use) the best styling tools for every job – and shows you what the professionals can't live without.

STYLING PRODUCTS

Styling products are the key to creating (and keeping) almost every look, from the simplest ponytail to the most elaborate updo. From fighting frizz to giving your hair more body, volume and shine, you'll find something here to fit the bill – along with a few ways to get the most out of whatever you choose.

Mousse

One of the most versatile styling aids of all, modern mousses are far from the stiff and sticky foams they once were. Primarily used for volume and hold, a good mousse can also fatten up fine hair, define curls, add shine and fight frizz. Formulations can vary to suit different hair types, as can the level of hold on offer. Extra benefits to look out for include protection from UV light (see page 28), conditioning properties, and colour-boosting or colour depositing (see page 54).

How to Use Mousse

• For volume and hold, most of the looks in this book benefit from a ball of mousse applied to the lengths and ends of freshly washed hair before styling. Apply after towel drying, while your hair is still damp but not dripping.
• As light and flexible as modern mousses are, avoid overapplying, or your hair could look stiff, flat and dirty. Start with a golf ball-sized amount, and add more if needed.

• Distribute your mousse by spreading it over your palms and fingers, smoothing it over your hair, and combing through with a wide-tooth comb.
• For extra volume, massage a small ball of mousse into your roots, flip your head forwards and direct the hot air from your dryer into the roots in a downwards direction before flipping back up and continuing to dry your hair as normal.
• Mousse can also be used to reboot the volume in dry hair. Massage into the roots and dry off with a hair dryer as above.

Hairspray

The effect of a hairspray can vary hugely, giving your hair anything from a natural, barely-there hold to a rock-firm finish. Lightweight formulations are useful for fighting frizz and can keep a simple blow-dry smooth and static free without affecting its softness and flexibility, while firm-hold hairsprays can help keep elaborate updos in place. Added extras vary from shine boosting to environmental protection, while some sprays can be used during styling (as well as afterwards) to give hold and definition right from the start and shield your hair from the extreme heat of curling tongs or straighteners.

How to Use Hairspray

• As well as misting directly onto your finished style, hairspray can also be applied with a brush (this helps you distribute your spray lightly, evenly and exactly where you need it), or with your fingers or hands (great for twisting through ends and tendrils or smoothing over the sides of a finished updo).
• Remember the difference between 'holding' or 'finishing' sprays and 'working' or 'styling' sprays.

Styling sprays can be used with heated tools and are great for prepping and setting hair during curling or straightening, or for building thickness into fine hair, while finishing sprays are used to hold finished looks in place.
• A lightweight spray with weather-protective properties can stop your hair from frizzing up or drooping down on humid or rainy days.
• Hairsprays can't build body, grip and malleability into your hair in the way that a mousse or thickening spray can. For the best results, use both.
• Some pump-action sprays can deposit their contents quite heavily onto the hair. Aerosols are often better for creating a light and continuous mist.
• Most hairsprays will brush easily out of your hair at the end of the day, avoiding product build-up and letting you start afresh the next day.

Product Build-up: Myth or Reality?

Most styling aids are formulated to avoid what's known as product build-up. They should wash (or even brush) cleanly out of your hair, leaving no residue behind. If your hair starts looking unusually limp or dull, try a clarifying or detoxing shampoo (see page 54), but also consider experimenting with a different brand of styling product, or trying a formulation that's been designed for your hair type. You may also be overapplying, so try not to get your products too close to your roots or use more than you really need (see page 44).

Shine Spray

Good gloss begins with the way you style, colour and care for your hair, but a gentle mist of a shimmering, light-reflective spray can create a patent-leather polish and control frizz and flyaways. Shine spray can also be quicker and easier to apply than a gloss-giving serum, especially on a finished updo that you don't want to dislodge – but a little can go a long way, so apply sparingly till you get to know your product.

How to Use Shine Spray

• Shine spray is a finishing product, so apply to dry hair as a last touch.

• Too much shine spray can leave your hair looking oily and flat, so avoid spraying directly onto your roots and keep the nozzle at least 15 centimetres from your hair.

• To avoid your roots, try spraying your product up into the air and walking through the mist it creates. Or flip your head forwards and spray into the mid-lengths and ends.

• If your hair is fine or flat, an oil-free formulation won't weigh it down as much as heavier sprays.

• If your hair is persistently dull, think about how your diet, environment or the way you care for and style your hair may be affecting its health (see pages 22–27).

Thickening Lotion

Used as an alternative to mousse, thickening lotions (also known as blow-dry lotions or sprays) build body, volume and texture into your hair for a fuller feel, and often have treatment properties that boost strength and condition. Like mousses, they should be worked through towel-blotted hair before blow-drying, but unlike mousse, they don't give your finished style quite as much texture and hold – softness and flexibility is their major attraction. Salt sprays also fall into this category – as well as thickening up your hair, they create a beachy and tousled texture, as if you've been swimming in the ocean and let you hair air-dry in the sea breeze.

How to Use Thickening Lotion

• For a lifted look without the all-over volume, lift damp hair section by section, spray directly into your roots and dry as usual.
• To thicken from root to tip, apply as above but continue to spray all the way down to the tips, or use your hands to scrunch and massage into the lengths and ends.
• Salt sprays will leave your hair looking matt rather than shiny. Break up the effect by twisting a dab of shine cream through a few selected mid-lengths and ends.
• Spritz salt sprays on damp or dry hair, then dry with a diffuser or leave it to dry naturally.

Five More Ways to Increase Fullness

• Have your hair coloured – hair dyes open up the cuticles on the surface and swell the hair shaft, making it thicker and creating more texture. A combination of highlights and lowlights can also create an optical illusion of thicker, fuller hair and gives your hair a lot more dimension and charm.
• Ask your hair stylist for a cut with more layers – this will get rid of some of the weight and make your hair seem thicker and more bouncy.
• If your hair is very limp, try applying your conditioner from just below your ears down to the ends. Keeping conditioner away from your roots will prevent it from dragging your hair down.
• Have your fringe cut, try a zigzag parting or get rid of your parting altogether (see page 66) – all of these will give the illusion of fuller hair.
• Backbrushing, backcombing (see page 82–85), and blow-drying (see page 74) all thicken your hair temporarily by roughing up the cuticles. Hanging your head upside down and blasting hot air up into your scalp will also make your hair look fuller by lifting it at the roots.

Dry Shampoo

Also known as hair powder, dry shampoo can be used to refresh hair between washes, create volume at the roots, give a deliberately matt, messy and lived-in look, and make freshly washed hair (which can be soft and slippery) easier to style. Once a backstage secret used at shoots and fashion shows, dry shampoo has been adopted by many different brands and is now widely available. Some create more of a matt and powdery look than others and can occasionally leave a white residue on darker hair, so experiment with a few different products until you find the right one.

How to Use Dry Shampoo
• Always apply to dry hair, lifting your hair up section by section and spraying into your roots and scalp.
• Leave to settle for a minute after application, to let the product soak up excess oil and moisture.
• Shake out any excess powder by brushing through with a natural bristle brush, or ruffling up your roots with your fingers.
• Create more volume by massaging the product into your roots after application, or try tipping your head forwards and blasting with a hair dryer.
• Most dry shampoos create a matt finish. If you prefer a glossier look, mist a shine spray over the top.

Gel

Hair gel has lost its dated image, and now does a lot more than create a wet-look finish. As well as the stronger formulations that keep short crops in place, gel is available in lightweight and creme-gel textures for defining curls and taming frizz in hair of any length. Formulations can be scooped out of pots and squeezed from bottles to apply by hand, or sprayed directly onto the roots.

How to Use Gel

• Most gels should be applied to damp hair, and left to dry naturally for a wet-look finish, or blow-dried for a drier, lighter look.

• If you're using gel to sculpt a shorter style, work while the hair is still wet, and blow-dry with your dryer on a slow speed, to set the look.

• Smooth lighter gels through longer hair for a sleek finish, or scrunch through to define curls.

• Unless you're creating a deliberately wet or slick look, gel should leave your hair looking natural rather than stiff, so don't overapply, and avoid getting gel on the very ends, unless you're trying to slick shorter styles down.

• Gel can also be used to define and hold specific sections of hair, such as a longer piece you're wrapping round the base of a ponytail.

• Try a dab of gel dried into the roots of longer hair to fight frizz around the hairline or keep a sleek updo in line.

Serum

This clear fluid comes into its own when you want a sleek, high-shine finish, and can be used to control frizz and flyaways, define curls and increase the impact of a straightened do. As serum coats the outside of the hair shaft, it can be useful in protecting your hair against the elements (especially if it contains a UV filter) or from the heat generated by electrical styling tools. Some also contain shimmer for a prettily glimmering effect.

How to Use Serum
• Rub the serum between your hands before you smooth it through your hair. This will warm it up and make it easier to distribute (especially if it contains silicones, which can build up unevenly if they're not applied correctly).
• Some serums can be hard to distribute when your hair is dry, so read the back of the bottle — you'll find that some should be applied to wet hair (after blotting and before blow-drying), while others can be smoothed over dry hair.
• Avoid applying serum too close to the roots, or your hair could look limp, greasy or flat — especially if it's already fine or naturally oily.
• Curly or thick hair can take more serum than straighter or finer types, so apply more as needed.

Five More Ways to Increase Shine

• Finish with a cold rinse when you wash your hair, to close down the cuticles and create a smooth and reflective surface.
• Blow-dry with a large, natural bristle barrel brush, pointing the nozzle down your hair shaft as you dry (see page 74).
• Look for straighteners with ceramic plates — as well as increasing shine, these work faster than metal plates and so don't damage your hair as much.
• Offset the drying effects of heated tools with a hair mask once a week. Look for ingredients such as jojoba or olive and coconut oils.
• Boost your intake of vitamin E and healthy fats (try nuts, coldwater fish, avocados and green leafy vegetables), and drink plenty of water to prevent your hair from becoming dehydrated, brittle, and dull.

Texturising Products

Pastes, putties, clays, muds and waxes all fall into this category, and are generally used in the final stages of the styling process, to create texture, define random ends, create a 'piecey' and separated effect, add polish and shine or create a matt and messy effect. They vary in hold, but as a general rule waxes are lighter, look softer and add shine, clays and putties give a stiffer, more textured feel, while fibrous pastes are heavier and sometimes stickier. They're ideal for shorter styles, but can look heavy and clumpy on longer hair types.

How to Use Texturising Products

• Many brands have a numbering system that shows you how much hold their product gives. These are particularly useful when choosing between all the different formulations.
• Always warm well before using by rubbing them into your palms or fingers until the friction melts the product and distributes it thinly and evenly over your skin.
• If your product contains fibres (the label on the pot may tell you), press and release your hands together before applying, to lengthen and thicken the fibres.
• Try twisting your fingers through the ends of random strands that you want to stand out. Start with a dab and add more as needed.
• Run your hands from side to side through shorter styles, to distribute evenly.

Styling Creams, Lotions and Balms

When waxes, putties and pastes are too heavy for longer hair, styling creams can be used instead, to define ends and create texture and separation. And when silicone-based serums overwhelm fine hair, a lightweight cream can take their place, to add shine and smooth the surface. Styling creams and lighter lotions are also a great option for defining fine curls that can droop when overloaded with mousse, while others have heat-protective properties and can be used before straightening and curling for softness, shine and manageability. Many are also conditioning and hydrating (think of them as moisturisers for your hair) and are perfect for drier and Afro hair types, as they can contain rich and nourishing ingredients such as shea butter.

How to Use Creams, Lotions and Balms
• Many styling creams can be applied to damp or dry hair, either by twisting them through the tips for separation, or smoothing them over the mid-lengths and ends for taming frizz and adding shine.
• To distribute cream evenly through longer hair, rub into your palms and fingers, pull back your hair as if you were creating a ponytail, twist it into a rope all the way down to the ends and then release.
• Straightening balms are applied to damp hair, and can tame frizzy hair by smoothing the cuticles. They are a great way to achieve a smooth sleek finish (see the Poker Straight look, page 134).
• As always, avoid overloading, and don't apply too close to the roots.

Thermal Protectors

Regular use of heated appliances can leave your hair feeling dry, looking lacklustre and prone to breakage. While all styling products protect your hair to some extent, simply by forming a barrier between it and the heat, many also have thermally protective properties (the packaging will tell you if this is the case). If not, you'll need to introduce some kind of protective step – especially if you're heating your hair on a daily basis. If you're layering on more than one product, make your thermal protector the last thing you apply before using your drier, curling tongs or straighteners. Simply spray on or smooth through with your fingers, working section by section to ensure an even application.

How to Use Thermal Protectors

• Keep your products to a minimum by looking for thermal protectors with other styling properties – for example, a volumising thermal spray may mean you can cut down on mousse, while a straightening serum can protect your hair before styling as well as adding shine.
• These products can be easier to apply section by section, so if you're curling or straightening your hair, spray or smooth your product through the section you're about to work on, rather than trying to distribute it through a whole head of hair before you start.

Pro Tips

• The cleaner your hair, the more product you'll need to create texture and hold.
• Applying your styling products in layers can increase thickness, texture and hold and stop you from overapplying. Apply once, blow-dry, apply another layer of product and dry again.
• If you're applying a styling product all the way through your hair rather than section by section, work it into the layers underneath and at the back of your head first. That way, by the time you get to the hair around your face and on top of your head, you'll have less product left on your fingers and will be less likely to overload where it'll be more visible. This works particularly well when you're applying finishing products to dry hair.

HOW MUCH PRODUCT?

Knowing how much styling product to apply is a matter of trial and error. Different hair types require different amounts – the more porous your hair, the more product it will suck up and the longer (and sometimes the cleaner) it is, the more product you'll need to achieve the lift, volume or staying power. In addition, the same type of product will vary from brand to brand, and you'll need more or less for different styles. So, until you're familiar with a formulation, start with a small amount and add more as needed.

Most products come with guidelines printed on the bottle, but here are some average amounts to get you started.

Mousse
A palmful or a golf ball-sized amount.

Gel
A squirt or scoop the size of a shelled walnut half.

Serum and Lotion
A pea-sized drop (this applies to anything liquid).

Balm and Cream
A squirt or scoop the size of a shelled almond.

Wax, Clay, Paste and Pomade
A scoop the size of a shelled almond.

Shampoo and Conditioner
A small puddle in the palm of your hand.

Pro Tip

Layering different products (or applying the same product in two separate coats) is a great way to achieve hold and texture, so don't feel you need to get everything from just one application. Try applying the first coat, drying it into your hair, applying a second coat and then drying again. This works particularly well with mousse, or with mousse and thickening spray.

Pro Tip

It's hard to turn back the clock once you've applied too much product. If you don't have the energy (or the time) to wash it out and start again, try spraying some dry shampoo into the roots, massaging it through your lengths and ends, and brushing it out again.

STYLING TOOLS

The right styling tools will help you create every look in this book. It's worth investing in the best you can afford, as really great tools will keep your hair looking healthy, shiny and strong, as well as give your styling efforts a professional edge – and they'll last a lifetime, too. Here are the ten key tools and simple accessories to start collecting.

Round Brush

With its flat oval shape and cushioned base, this all-purpose brush smoothes hair of any length without knocking out its natural volume. It is the best choice for simple techniques such as backbrushing or guiding hair into updos, extensions and general detangling.

Pro Tips

- Look after your natural bristle brushes by teasing out any loose hair with a comb, washing them in warm water with a squirt of shampoo, rinsing well and leaving to dry naturally.
- Thermal or ceramic brushes are designed to hold the heat from your dryer and conduct it back into your hair, increasing the speed and efficiency of your blow-dry. If you have dry, fragile or chemically treated hair, these may be best avoided, as they can increase the potentially damaging effects of the drying process.
- To give an updo an undone look, put your hair up with your hands instead of using a brush.

Barrel Brush

This helps you blow-dry your hair to a smooth, sleek finish, and is great for creating a look that's curled, turned under or flicked out at the ends. A larger barrel will create a looser curl or more lift, and is also better for longer hair, while a smaller barrel will give less lift and a tighter curl, and suits shorter styles.

Paddle Brush

The wide, flat shape of this brush makes it perfect for detangling longer, thicker hair, and for blow-drying straight styles that need no lift or volume.

Natural or Synthetic Bristles?

While natural bristle brushes can be expensive, they're worth investing in for the smooth and shiny finish they give your hair, without tearing any strands or irritating your scalp. However, nylon bristles (which are tougher than natural ones) can be better at grabbing onto the hair and taming tangles, so a brush with a mix of both is often the best bet, especially if you have normal to thick hair. Plastic bristles don't have the same shine-giving, static-taming properties as natural, and if there are tiny bobbles on the tips, make sure they're part of the bristles rather than stuck onto the ends, so they can't fall off and expose a sharp point that could tear your hair or scratch your scalp. Avoid using brushes with metal pins while blow-drying, as they can conduct too much heat into the hair.

Wide-tooth Comb

Brushes can pull and damage wet hair, so a wide-tooth comb is helpful for detangling after washing and for combing through conditioner. Avoid combs with rough seams, as these can catch on your hair, and check that the teeth have smoothly rounded ends, so they don't scratch your scalp.

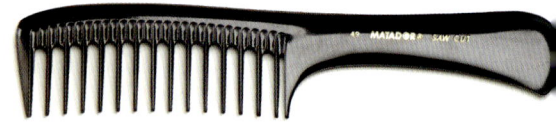

Pintail Comb

With a long thin handle for creating sections and partings and fine teeth for precision styling at the other end, a pintail comb is an essential prepping tool.

Sectioning Clips

A few of these will make styling so much easier with your hair. Use them to hold large sections out of the way so you can see exactly what you're doing and won't get your tools tangled up. A few long, flat, silver clips can also be useful for setting waves in place.

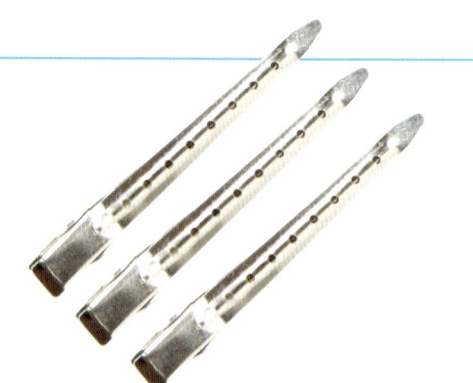

Kirby Grips

Probably one of the cheapest but most essential hair accessories around, you can never have too many of them. From pinning a chignon in place to tidying away a single strand, there's little they can't do.

Pro Tip

Buy grips that are as close as possible to your hair colour (they're usually available in gold, black and brown) and build up a collection of different lengths, to help hold a range of styles in place.

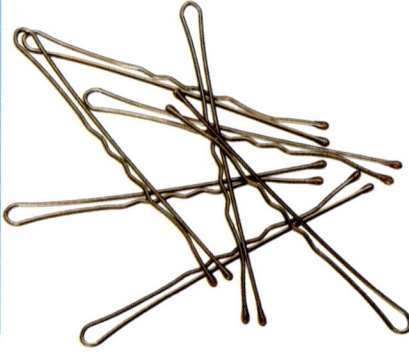

Hair Elastics

Essential for fastening ponytails and plaits in place, the best elastics are made of smooth, seamless plastic, so they don't add bulk and won't snag and damage your hair. The added bonus of these elastics is that they come in neutral shades of black and brown or are completely clear, so give simple styles a grown-up tone.

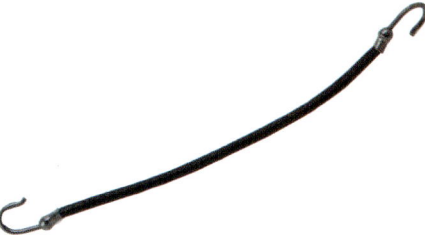

Bungee Bands

An alternative to classic bands, bungees are straight hair elastics that have a hook at either end. These can be wrapped around the base of a ponytail to hold the hair as tightly or loosely as you like, and are great at keeping a lot of hair firmly in position.

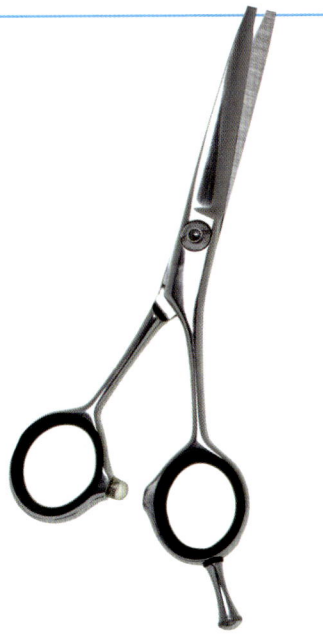

Hair Scissors

Cutting your own hair or trimming your fringe isn't for the fainthearted, but if you're going to try it, make sure you use a pair of hair-specific scissors, not something you've pulled from a kitchen drawer. The blades will be light, sharp and fine, and the handles designed for maximum comfort and a nonslip grip.

ELECTRICAL TOOLS

The best way to create long-lasting looks and temporarily change the texture of your hair is to bend it into shape when it's warm and let it cool to set – this is where heated styling tools come in. Because regular exposure to intense temperatures can weaken and damage your hair, it's worth buying tools that work as quickly as possible and allow you to manipulate their temperatures as needed.

Hair Dryer

The best dryers allow you to vary the heat and speed of your airflow. The lower settings are useful for gently drying off partings and shorter styles without dislodging them, while the higher settings will help you blast your hair after towel drying, so you can get rid of a lot of water before you switch to a medium heat for a smooth, sleek blow-dry.

Pro Tips

- Ionic dryers (these send out air that's loaded with more negative than positive ions) can help speed up the drying process and give your hair a sleeker finish. They hydrate your hair by breaking down the water droplets on it so they can be absorbed back into the strands, as well as evaporating into the air. You may find you have to spend a lot of money before you get one that really makes a difference, so try getting to know the heat and speed settings on your regular dryer first. Make sure your model has between 1,600 and 1,800 watts – this should dry your hair efficiently without blowing it out of control.
- Other extras to consider are a cold shot button (which can help set curls in place), a range of nozzles or a diffuser (for drying naturally curly or wavy hair without frizz), and also think about whether you find the grip comfortable and the controls easy to manipulate while you style.

Curling Tongs

These are used for creating ringlet-style curls that can be tweaked into flowing waves or looser tousles. The larger the barrel, the looser and larger the curl you'll get from it, while tapered or conical tongs will aid longevity and add a tapered end to the bottom of the curl. A temperature setting will help you vary the heat as needed (around 200°F should be high enough), and a ceramic barrel will hold and conduct the heat faster and more evenly than any other material.

Pro Tip

Curling tongs with clamps are useful for holding the hair firmly in place while you wind the tongs up towards your roots. However, the clamp can dent the ends of your hair and create a kink. If you'd rather wind your hair round the tongs with your fingers (this is the way many professionals work, though it can be fussy), choose tongs without a clamp (a curling wand). A clamp that you can hold open while you work gives you the best of both worlds.

Pro Tips

- A pair of mini-irons can help you straighten fluffy wisps around your hairline and the nape of your neck, and are great for a fringes and short crops.
- Straighteners with curved backs can be used to curl the hair as well as straighten it, and are great for turning ends underneath to help the hair hang with a slight curve.

Straighteners

These give a flatter, sleeker finish than even the smoothest blow-dry. They are also helpful for ironing smaller sections, to give an overall groomed look. Look for straighteners with longer, slimmer plates made of ceramic rather than metal, as these are easier to slide through the hair, and will conduct the heat more evenly, so you shouldn't have to iron the same section more than once. As with curling tongs, straighteners with a temperature setting will allow you to find the best heat for your hair type.

Chapter 3

ESSENTIAL TECHNIQUES

As well as exploring everyday hair-care techniques such as washing and drying, this chapter will give you the building blocks you'll need to create every style in this book.

WASHING, CONDITIONING AND HEAD MASSAGING

Washing well and conditioning correctly can protect your colour, boost shine and volume, and help prepare your hair for styling, as well as giving you the opportunity to care for its health.

Stronger, Softer, Brighter – Which Hair Care Should You Choose?

The right shampoo and conditioner will keep your hair and scalp happy and healthy, and can work hand in hand with your styling products to help you build a look from the word go.

Colour-boosting

Colour-reviving shampoo, conditioner and hair masks work in different ways, depending on your shade (and most will work on natural or chemically coloured hair). Some deposit a small number of colour particles onto the hair to keep it looking rich and vibrant, while others keep fair hair looking bright with gently lightening ingredients, such as citrus extracts, and also remove colour-dulling impurities and neutralise brassy yellow tones. Most make colour seem stronger by boosting shine and usually have deeply conditioning properties, to repair hair that may have been damaged and dehydrated by chemical processing.

Volumising

As well as increasing strength, volumising shampoos gently cleanse away any residues that might weigh the hair down and pull moisture into the hair, to swell the diameter and make it temporarily thicker. They can also coat the outside of every hair with polymers and proteins, which encourages the strands to stand further away from one another and take up more space. The formulations of volumising conditioners are usually lighter and leave fewer residues, so moisturise without dragging the hair down.

Clarifying

Clarifying shampoos are designed to clean your hair of all the things that can leave it looking limp, dull and dirty (natural oils, styling products or heavy pollution) but can also cause dehydration and even strip away your colour. Don't use them more than once a week, and do try to counter their potentially damaging effects with a good conditioner or mask.

Anti-ageing

With age (and the hormonal changes that come with it), hair can become dry, dull, thin and fragile, and less able to cope with the wear and tear of daily styling. Anti-ageing hair care has glossing ingredients to restore lustre, and proteins, vitamins

Pro Tips

- If you're creating a look for a special occasion, think of your shampoo and conditioner as an extension of your styling routine. If you're planning a poker-straight look, use a frizz-fighting or extra-moisturising shampoo, or conditioner, or both. If you want a bouncier-than-usual blow-dry, or a look with extra height at the crown, try a volumising duo.
- The best hair masks will contain moisturising ingredients such as nut and seed oils and butters, and strengthening ingredients such as proteins, amino acids and panthenol (vitamin B5).
- If you don't have time to let a moisturising mask sink in, try using it as an intensive conditioner – just apply as you would your regular conditioner, gently comb through and rinse out.

rather than rough and dull. If these formulas feel too heavy for your hair, mix and match them with lighter products, or keep them away from your roots.

Oil-controlling

The oilier your hair and scalp, the more dirt and debris they will attract on a daily basis, making regular cleansing increasingly important. However, washing away too many of the natural oils can increase sebum production and dehydrate the hair, leaving it looking limp, dull and even oilier. The best shampoos clear oily scalps without stripping or overstimulating, and are mild enough to use regularly, while the conditioners rehydrate without overloading. They often contain scalp-toning and sebum-regulating ingredients such as seaweed extracts, tea tree, rosemary and zinc, and can boost root-lift and fullness too.

Hair Masks and Overnight Treatments

Conditioning and strengthening hair treatments have a greater concentration of nourishing ingredients than regular conditioners, and are designed to sit on the hair for anywhere up to twenty minutes, leaving the cuticles smooth and flat and the hair soft, shiny and protected. They can usually be used up to once a week, and come in the form of masks that moisturize, or strengthen, or both, and hot oil treatments. Newer to the market are overnight treatments, which provide your hair with a drip-feed of moisturising and strengthening ingredients over a longer period of time. Some need to be washed out in the morning, while others sink in completely.

and minerals to boost density and strength. It can also soothe and hydrate the scalp, which can become sensitive as sebum production decreases.

Moisturising, Shine-enhancing and Frizz-fighting

Shampoos and conditioners that hydrate, repair and smooth the hair usually contain a combination of ingredients such as aloe vera, jojoba, coconut, avocado and nut butters and oils, and silicones to fight static and frizz. The detergents may be milder than in other formulations, and both the shampoo and conditioner will close the cuticles on the outside of the hair, so the surface is smooth and reflective

This hair mask is for when your hair is in need of intensive repair.

How to Wash Your Hair

step 1

Brush or comb your hair before washing, especially if it's long – tangles are harder to remove when your hair is wet.

➜ step 2

When your hair is wet through (the wetter your hair, the better your product will travel down the lengths) apply your shampoo, focusing on the roots and working your way down (see page 44 for a guide to product amounts).

◐ step 3

Massage the soft pads of your fingers into your scalp in small circles. This will help emulsify the product, lift away any dirt and oil, and stimulate blood flow.

How Often Should You Wash?

Different hair types have different needs, and those needs may change with lifestyle and environment. For most people, washing three times a week should be enough. Oily hair may need washing more often than dry hair, but if you over-massage your scalp or use very hot water, you may stimulate oil production and end up needing to wash even more often. Changes in humidity may prompt more frequent washing, as oil production can increase in humid conditions, making your hair seem limp and flat. Signs that you're washing too often may include a flaky scalp, brittle ends and hair prone to static. Massaging the scalp too often or too vigorously can overstimulate sebaceous glands which can produce too much oil onto the scalp, resulting in greasy hair. Washing too little may leave your hair looking lank and oily or feeling lifeless.

⊕ step 4

Rinse until the water runs completely clear, then blot your hair with a towel to prevent too much water from diluting your conditioner.

⊕ step 5

Apply your conditioner, focusing more on the mid-lengths and ends, and less on your roots, which need less oil than the rest of your hair and tend to suffer from less damage.

step 6

Leave your conditioner in for anything from a few seconds to a couple of minutes, then rinse till the water runs clear.

↑ step 7

Gently wring the water from your hair by squeezing it with alternate fists, working your way from the roots right down to the ends.

↑ step 8

Blot with a towel (rubbing dry can rub up the cuticles, damage your hair and leave it looking rough and dull) and wrap it up on top of your head.

Shampoo and Conditioner: What Does What?

A shampoo's job is to break down and lift up the film of dirt, sebum and dead skin cells that collects on the hair and scalp, so it can be rinsed away with water. At the same time, the shampoo will deposit some lightly conditioning ingredients onto the hair. Some formulations offer additional benefits such as colour protection or extra volume and shine, but the main priority is that the detergents don't damage or dehydrate the hair by destroying its natural pH balance. Conditioners are oil-based creams and lotions that coat the hair shaft and encourage the cuticles to lie flat. This increases shine, decreases porosity and protects the hair from further damage. The ingredients in more intensive conditioners can also penetrate a little way into the hair, to fill any weakened areas, making the hair stronger and more supple.

Pro Tip Dos and Don'ts

Do...

... use as mild a shampoo as possible. The gentler the detergents in the formulation, the less it will strip or dehydrate your hair, and the less you'll have to rely on your conditioner or styling products to keep your hair looking healthy.

... wash your hair in lukewarm water. Scorching temperatures can damage and dehydrate your hair, eventually leaving it dull and brittle.

... apply more conditioner to your ends (which are the oldest bits of your hair and so can be drier and more damaged) and keep it away from your roots (which can be weighed down by too much product).

... consider changing your hair care if your upper back, chest or shoulders suddenly break out in blemishes. The product that's rinsing out of your hair and over your skin could be causing an irritation.

Don't ...

... add more shampoo just because it's not frothing up enough (some brands now contain fewer frothing agents because they're said to damage the hair). To create more foam, try adding more water.

... always shampoo twice with every wash. A good shampoo should wash your hair well without a second cleanse, especially if you're using the right formulation for your hair type.

... use conditioner if you don't really need it – especially if your hair is short.

... forget that the richer, thicker and more moisturising or shine-boosting your shampoo is, the more likely it is to overload your hair or weigh it down. If this is becoming a problem, try alternating with something lighter.

Head Massage

Massaging your scalp while you wash your hair helps to work conditioner deep into the hair and along the shaft. It will also help stimulate blood flow to encourage healthy hair growth and scalp condition, and can be a great way to release tension. Try a combination of the following techniques, for anything up to ten minutes.

⊙ step 1

Keeping the soft pads of your fingers in the same place, so you're moving your scalp rather than just moving your fingers, circle your hands first one way and then the next.

step 2

Repeat with your thumbs, moving from place to place over your scalp before circling back and forth.

Pro Tips

- Increase or decrease the pressure depending on how sensitive your scalp is – scalp massage should never leave you with a headache!
- Try starting gently, increasing the pressure and intensity, and then decreasing again.
- These techniques can also be used when your hair is dry, to boost blood flow and help destress at any time of day.

➔ step 3

Run your knuckles quickly and lightly back and forth over your scalp.

◀ step 4

Finish by gently running your fingers over your scalp and through your hair, gently removing any tangles at the same time.

SECTIONING

Sectioning is one of the most helpful prepping skills to have under your styling belt – knowing how to divide your hair into workable portions can make potentially tricky techniques such as curling and straightening so much easier, while the right parting can change the look of an updo in one simple stroke.

Horizontal Sectioning

Dividing your hair into horizontal sections has three main benefits when styling: it gets the bulk of your hair out of the way so you can see exactly what you're doing; you won't get your tools tangled up in free-floating lengths while you work; and you'll be working on finer sections of hair at a time, so your styling products and heated tools will work faster and more efficiently.

step 1

Decide how many sections you'll need to divide your hair into. Most of the step-by-step styling instructions in this book recommend two or three, but if your hair is particularly thick or curly, you may want to introduce extra horizontal bands by creating more divisions.

➋ step 2

Create your top section before moving down to the next. The part that creates a top section usually runs from temple to temple, or sits right on the top of your head, starting and finishing at the end of either eyebrow (this is known as a D-section or half-moon).

step 3

Part your hair by sliding the thin end of a pintail comb horizontally along your scalp, under the hair. Then move the comb away from your head so it gently parts your hair. Use your fingers to gather up all the hair above the comb.

← step 4

Twist the hair you've gathered in your fingers into a coil and fasten it firmly and cleanly out of the way, using a sectioning clip on either side of the knot.

step 5

If you're creating another section below the one you've just made, repeat as above, guiding the hair towards the back of your head rather than up on top, before clipping it out of the way. The part for this lower section will often run from ear to ear.

Product Tip

Crocodile clips (pictured) are great for holding a lot of hair as their design means hair doesn't snag.

D-section or Half-moon

• A D-section or half-moon is the section that sits on the very top of your head. It could be the upper section of two or three (as described in the sequence above), or if you're creating a style such as a chignon or French plait or preparing to trim a fringe, it could be the only section you'll need.

• The part that creates a D-section or half-moon usually starts and ends directly above the tail end of each eyebrow, but can be as deep or shallow as you need – the deeper it is, the further back it will go and the more hair it will pick up.

• If you're trimming your fringe, you'll use a shallower half-moon, while the D-section used for creating quiffs, chignons and French plait can be much deeper, depending on how much hair you want to work with.

Pro Tip

Using kirby grips as a guideline can help you create a section that runs in a straight line all the way around your head. Holding one finger on the point at which you're going to start sectioning, slip a brightly coloured grip (that will stand out rather than disappear into your hair) into your hairline at the same point on the opposite side of your head. This gives you something to aim for as you work your way around.

Partings

The right parting can flatter your face shape (see page 224) and change the look of a style or cut. Creating your parting with a pintail comb will give it a crisper, cleaner feel, but you can also use your fingers for a more effortless and undone look.

Straight Parting

A classic straight parting can be positioned in the centre or to one side, and can look crisp and neat, or softly tousled if you use your fingers.

Curved Parting

A curved parting can create a softer look than a classic straight parting.

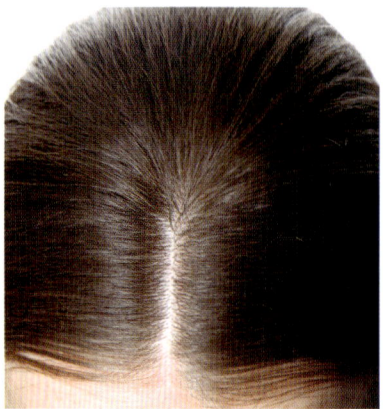

Reduced Parting

Reduced partings can sit in the middle or to one side, and are great for creating updos that need height at the back.

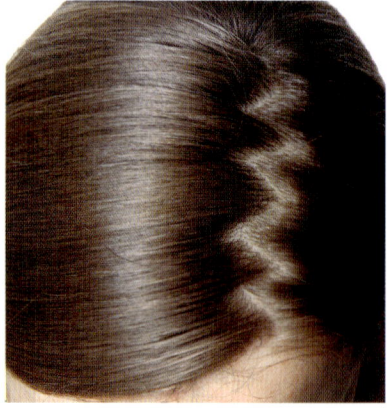

Zigzag Parting

A zigzag parting can help to disguise greying roots, or a colour that's started to grow out. It can also make hair look fuller, and lend any look a more modern feel.

Creating a Parting

step 1

Decide where your parting will sit.

step 2

Slide the fine end of your pintail comb along your scalp and horizontally into your hair, until it's lying flat against your head.

step 3

Start to lift the comb up through your hair, still holding it horizontally.

step 4

Use your fingers to separate the hair off your comb to reveal your parting.

step 5

Smooth the hair into position with your hands, and comb through to finish.

Pro Tips

- To create a curved parting, follow the instructions for the straight parting but move the comb in a semicircular line from the front to the back.
- To create a zigzag parting, wiggle the tip of the pintail comb from side to side as you glide it over the scalp, then when you reach the finishing point for your parting, use both hands to separate hair either side to reveal your zigzag.
- Partings that are created when your hair is wet or damp will always look less severe as your hair dries, unless you're working with a lot of product.
- Some styles look more modern with no parting at all – try pulling your hair back from your hairline with either your fingers or a brush.
- Try a deep side parting (positioned low on one side of your head, a few centimetres above the ear) and pull your hair softly back into a low bun or ponytail.
- Try a reduced centre parting, backbrush the roots of the hair behind it and pull the hair into a high bun or ponytail, for height and volume at the back.
- Try a side parting to balance out a low, looped side ponytail by positioning it on the opposite side of your head.
- Try a centre parting before pulling your hair back into an updo, but let your hair fall softly over your ears, rather than pulling it tightly behind them, for a demure and retro look.
- To find the place where your parting naturally falls (this will always be the easiest parting to work with, and will require less product to keep in place), comb your hair straight back from your forehead, then shake it forwards over your face, or place your hand on the back of your head and move it firmly up your scalp and over the top, pushing your hair until it rises up from your scalp.
- If you style your hair repeatedly in the same parting, you'll find your hair begins to fall naturally in that position.

DRYING YOUR HAIR

There are so many different ways to dry your hair, depending on how much time you have, how co-operative your hair is, and what sort of effect you want to achieve. Hair that falls easily into place can be left to dry naturally or given a short, sharp blast, but for shine, manageability, volume and texture, it's worth mastering the art of the blow-dry.

The Rough Dry

Blow-drying with your hands is a great way of styling weak and chemically treated hair or shorter styles, and comes into its own when you're in a hurry. It will save time and effort, and decreases the amount of potential damage created by the tugging and pulling of the hairbrush. You can use this technique to get most of the moisture out of your hair before you start blow-drying with a brush, to create a sleeker look.

step 1	step 2	step 3
Get the drying process off to a good start by blotting your hair with a towel.	Smooth your chosen styling product through your hair — choose mousse for volume or serum for a sleeker, straighter effect.	Set your dryer to a medium heat and a high-speed setting, and begin to dry your hair, always making sure the airflow is travelling down the hair shaft from root to tip.

step 4

Comb your hair with your fingers as it dries, lifting and separating to allow the hot air to circulate.

step 5

If you're preparing your hair for a full blow-dry, stop when your hair is 80 per cent dry.

Pro Tips

• Blotting your hair with your towel rather than rubbing it contributes to a sleeker finish, as it smoothes down the cuticles on the surface of the hair instead of ruffling them up the wrong way. Start by pressing the towel gently but firmly over your scalp and then sandwich it around the lengths of your hair, working from your roots down to the ends, pressing and squeezing out the water.

• While rough drying is a versatile and effective way to style your hair, it won't help you to create precise effects such as a poker-straight look, or a head full of defined curls. For more on blow-drying, see pages 74–81.

step 6

If you're continuing to rough dry, use your hands to create texture, volume and shape…

• Create volume at the roots by lifting sections of hair up and away from your head and directing the airflow upwards from root to tip as you dry.

• Create texture by scrunching your fingers into your hair while it's still warm from the dryer and holding it loosely in your fist as it cools.

• Create curls by twisting your hair around your fingers as you dry. Hold while the hair cools, then release.

• Straighten your hair by smoothing your fingers through each section and gently pulling and lengthening as you dry.

step 7

Let your hair cool and set, then apply a light hairspray to fix in place.

Drying Short Hair

An easy guide to getting volume and definition into short styles without leaving them looking stiff or unnatural.

Pro Tools
- Hair dryer
- Light- or medium-hold hairspray
- Lightweight wax

Pro Techniques
- Defining ends

Pro Prep
- Work mousse through damp hair for volume and control.

➔ step 1
Create lift in the top and front sections by holding your hair above your head as you dry it, pointing the nozzle upwards, and directing the hot air from root to tip.

➔ step 2
For a sleeker look, pull the hair down and direct the hot air down the hair shaft.

⊖ step 3

To create a loose and natural texture, ruffle your fingers from side to side through the top section as you dry it, working in fast movements closely over the scalp.

step 4

Twist a light dab of soft wax through the ends and spray with light- or medium-hold hairspray to fix.

Product Tip

You could try using a sea salt spray instead of the mousse to create a textured finish.

Drying Curly Hair

The bonus of natural curls is having the kind of volume and body that those with straighter hair types can only dream about, especially when cut well and defined with the right products.

How to Dry Curly Hair

Curly hair can respond beautifully to a straight blow-dry, as long as you coat it with a serum while it's still wet, and always remember to point the hot air down the hair shaft from root to tip.

Pro Tips

- To avoid frizz, let your hair dry naturally for as long as possible before beginning to blow-dry.
- If you're sticking with your natural texture, try coating damp hair with a leave-in conditioner and gently scrunching and cupping your curls in your hands as you dry with a diffuser.

Air-drying can also work well on natural curls – try running a generous amount of leave-in conditioner through damp hair and leaving it to dry naturally.

Pro Tips

- Don't waste your time straightening naturally curly hair in a hot and humid climate – it will revert to type the minute you step outside, leaving you with a headful of frizz. Instead, embrace your curls and keep them looking sleek by applying a leave-in conditioner or a silicone-based styling product, such as a serum, before styling, making sure you coat every curl.
- Soft updos, such as ballerina buns, often look better on curly hair types than styles that are tightly pulled back, as they give the natural texture a chance to shine.

To add shine and define your curls without flattening them, work a pomade or light wax gently through the very top layers.

You can enhance your curls further by coiling them around your fingers and then gently releasing them. Allow them to dry naturally or under a diffuser.

Blow-dry Basic Technique

Co-ordinating your dryer and brush can feel awkward at first, but practice will make perfect.

Product Tips

- To give your hair even more texture, thickness and grip, apply a second coat of mousse between rough drying and blow-drying.
- Or, for a sleeker finish, use serum instead of mousse, smoothing it through towel-blotted hair while it's still quite damp.
- Choose styling products with thermal protection, especially if you blow-dry your hair on a regular basis.

⬆ step 1

Sleek strokes from root to tip are the key to a smooth blow-dry. Move down the hair without stopping, brushing from underneath and following closely with the dryer from above, so the hot air always hits the hair that's wrapped over the top of the brush.

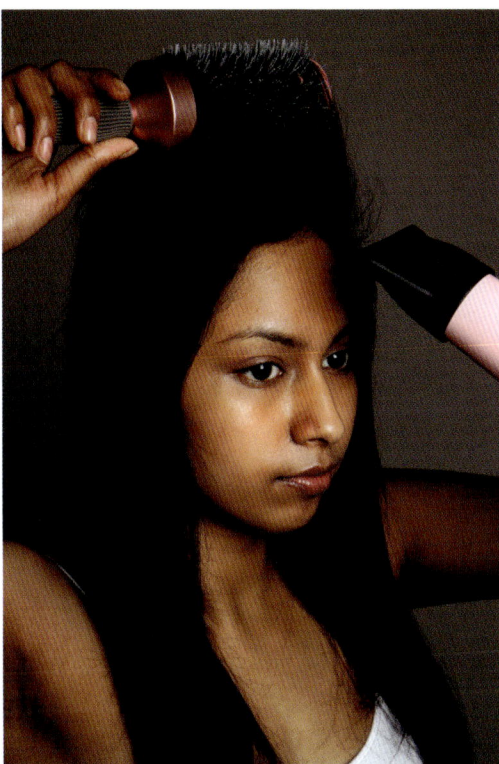

⬅ step 2

When finishing off your fringe or the hair around your face, pull the hair up as you brush, to build volume and smooth the underside of the sections.

Pro Tips

- Working on sections no larger than a couple of centimetres wide will make your hair easier to handle and help it to dry faster.
- Keep your dryer on a medium-heat, high-speed setting and hold the nozzle a couple of centimetres away from the surface of the hair.
- Always direct the airflow along the hair shaft from root to tip, so the hot air smoothes the cuticles flat rather than roughing them up the other way.
- Using a mirror may confuse you at first, as your mirror image will be doing everything from back to front. Until you've perfected the technique, use the mirror to get your brush in position and then look away as you pull your brush down through your hair.

Blow-drying for Different Looks

Knowing how to handle a hair dryer will give your day-to-day look a professional edge. Once you've mastered the basic technique, you'll be able to vary your blow-dry style – from curly and voluminous to sleek and straight.

Pro Tools
- Pintail comb
- Sectioning clips
- Natural bristle barrel brush
- Mousse
- Hairspray

Pro Techniques
- Sectioning
- Rough drying

Pro Prep
- Smooth mousse from root to tip after towel drying.
- Rough dry on a high speed and heat until your hair is between 70 and 80% dry.
- Use a pintail comb to create two or three sections (this will depend on how thick your hair is) and clip all but the bottom section out of the way.

↑ step 1

Working with sections that are a couple of centimetres wide, gently glide your brush from root to tip, brushing from underneath and following with the dryer from above. Repeat until the hair feels dry and looks smooth, and then move on to the next section. Work your way around your head until you reach the other side.

⬆ step 2

Once the bottom section is smooth and sleek, unclip the section above and repeat.

⬆ step 3

Move on to the top layers and the sections around your face. Make sure these are the smoothest and sleekest of all by drying first from above and then from underneath.

For Ends That Curl Under

⬆
Pull the brush straight back down and out at the ends.

⬆
As you reach the end of each section, roll the brush halfway back up the section and hold the brush in position until it cools, before continuing to dry.

For a Straight Finish

⬆
Use a larger barrel brush or a paddle brush for an even flatter look, and glide it straight through each section rather than curling the ends under.

⬆
For an even sleeker finish, switch your dryer to a hotter setting when you dry the surface layers and move the nozzle slowly from side to side as you follow the brush down to the end.

For a Curlier Blow-dry

⬆

Just before you reach the ends, roll the brush right back into the roots and hold it in place for between thirty seconds and a minute. Direct the hot air away from your head so the hair on the brush can cool down, or use the cold shot button to speed up the setting process.

⬆

Unwind the brush from your hair by rotating your wrist in circles and moving your hand downwards, so the brush twists down and out of the hair.

step 4

Mist with hairspray to hold.

Pro Tips

- A barrel brush will help lift your hair at the roots, or try a flat paddle brush for a volume-free look.
- A combination of natural and nylon bristles will boost shine as well as gripping onto your hair and helping smooth out any tangles.
- A thermal or ceramic brush will help you dry your hair faster, but can also get too hot for dry or fragile hair types.
- Use a bigger barrel brush on longer hair, or to create a smoother, flatter finish, and a smaller one for shorter styles or to create curls.

TEXTURISING TECHNIQUES

Used to give your hair body, volume and height, or to create a modern, messed-up effect, texturising techniques such as backbrushing, finger-teasing and defining ends are crucial for building foundations and finishing off a look. Or, for a dramatic change, try curling with tongs or creating a smooth and glassy finish with straighteners.

Backcombing

Pro Tools
- Fine-tooth comb
- Hairspray

Also known as teasing, backcombing creates body, lift and volume by pushing your hair in an opposite direction to its natural growth pattern and roughing up the cuticles, making it temporarily thicker. It creates a bigger base for an updo, and can also give fine or freshly washed hair (which can be too soft and slippery to hold a style) a better texture to work with.

Use backcombing to:
- Build volume at the roots of any style;
- Create a quiff;
- Bulk up a chignon or the front of a French plait;
- Build volume at the back of the head for a beehive-inspired shape;
- Provide a secure base for grips or temporary extensions to be secured into.

step 1	step 2
Make sure your hair is clean, dry and (if you've just straightened, curled or blow-dried your hair) cool.	Isolate the area you want to build body into by creating a half-moon or D-section (if you're building body on top) or just clipping the rest of the hair out of the way of the roots you're trying to reach.

step 3

Taking one section of hair at a time (try a few centimetres in thickness to start with, but work on finer sections if you want to create even more volume), hold the hair firmly above or out to the side of your head until it's straight and taut.

 step 4

Push the comb down from a few centimetres away from your scalp right into your roots in short, brisk strokes – the comb will push some but not all of the hair down into the roots to create a pillow of fine, fluffy strands.

Pro Tips

- Because backcombing gives the surface of the hair a rougher texture, it can also be used to create extra 'grip' when you want a heavy kirby grip or other accessory to stay in place.
- Try spraying your backcombed sections as you go; this will give them more hold and longevity.

step 5

When you've backcombed the section in your hand, let it go and move onto the next.

step 6

Mist with hairspray and style into position.

Backbrushing

Pro Tools
- Natural bristle brush
- Hairspray

Like backcombing, backbrushing roughs up the cuticles on the surface of the hair, making it thicker and fuller. While backcombing is great for texturising smaller sections and getting volume right into the roots, backbrushing is better for building body into a large area of hair. It also creates a pretty lived-in or fluffed-up texture, and can help break up curls that look too pristine.

Use backbrushing to:
- Build volume into longer lengths;
- Fatten up a ponytail before twisting it into an oversized bun;
- Give curled hair a soft and fluffy texture;
- Boost volume in long hair from underneath.

step 1

Isolate the area of hair you want to backbrush by sectioning it off or clipping the rest of the hair out of the way.

➔ step 2

Working on small-medium size sections at a time, hold the sections out from the top or side of your head until they're taut.

↑ step 3

Brush the hair backwards from the tips down into the roots, until you've brushed all the hair in your hand down onto your head in a voluminous cloud.

↑ step 4

Guide your hair back into the required style, smoothing the outer layers down with the bristles of your brush. Mist with hairspray to hold.

Pro Tips

- All teasing techniques leave hair looking fluffy and matt. If you want your finished style to look sleek and shiny, smooth the top layer of backcombed or backbrushed hair with a natural bristle brush, but be careful not to disturb the body underneath.
- To remove any tangles left by a vigorous bout of backcombing or backbrushing, take fine sections of hair and work through the knots with a natural bristle brush.
- To avoid ripping your hair, work through the knots from the bottom to the top rather than from top to bottom. Hold your hair a few centimetres above the tips and work on clearing the knots in the ends first. When this section is fully untangled, move up the hair shaft and work on the next few centimetres. Repeat till you reach your roots.
- Always untangle teased hair before you wash it – it's far harder to remove knots when the hair is wet.
- Treat frequently teased hair to regular deep-conditioning masks and protein treatments.

Finger-teasing

Pro Tools
- Hairspray

Used to texturise single strands and random tendrils, this technique lends a lived-in look to styles that might otherwise seem too stiff. It can give free-flowing lengths an extra bit of structure and definition, and is a flattering way of framing your face after pulling your hair back into an updo.

step 1

Take small sections of hair from your almost finished look, either by gently pulling them away from an updo, or by picking them randomly out of loose lengths if you're wearing your hair down.

⬆ step 3

Push your finger and thumb up toward the roots, so some of the strands bunch up to create a deliberately frizzed effect.

step 4

Repeat step 3, working in a combination of long and short upward strokes. Release and move onto the next strand.

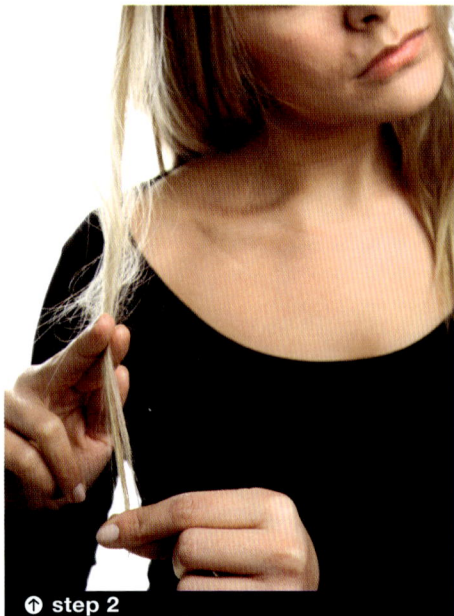

⬆ step 2

Holding the end of the section tightly in one hand, pull it out to one side so it's straight and taut, then use the finger and thumb of your other hand to grip the strand firmly, a few centimetres up from the tips.

step 5

When you've created enough volume and texture, mist the strands with hairspray to hold.

Separating Curls

Pro Tools
- Natural bristle brush

Breaking up a head of freshly curled hair with your fingers and a brush can turn a cascade of perfectly formed ringlets into a cloud of soft curls, and give them a more natural look.

➜ step 1
Use your fingertips to gently split and then pull your curls apart, working from top to bottom.

step 2
Use a natural bristle brush to gently brush through the curls, holding them against your hand as you brush, so you don't pull down too roughly and stretch out the shape.

← step 3
To create even more volume and texture, try gently backbrushing the curls from underneath, before smoothing over the top with your brush.

step 4
Mist with hairspray to hold.

Pro Tips
- Breaking up curls by pulling them gently apart with your fingertips, rather than dragging your hands through them, helps loosen the texture without losing the shape.
- You can also give fresh curls a looser texture by pulling the ends down between your finger and thumb while the curls are still warm. This will stretch and lengthen them while they're still setting.

Defining Ends

Pro Tools

- Texturising wax, putty or styling cream

Like finger-teasing, twisting a styling product through a few random ends can break up a look that might otherwise seem too solid. This can give longer hair a 'piecey' finish, define any strands you've pulled out of an updo to frame your face, and add interest and height to shorter styles.

step 1

Work a dab of wax, styling cream, putty or pomade between your thumb and your first two fingers – unless you've just worked some product through the mid-lengths of your hair, in which case you may have enough on your fingers already.

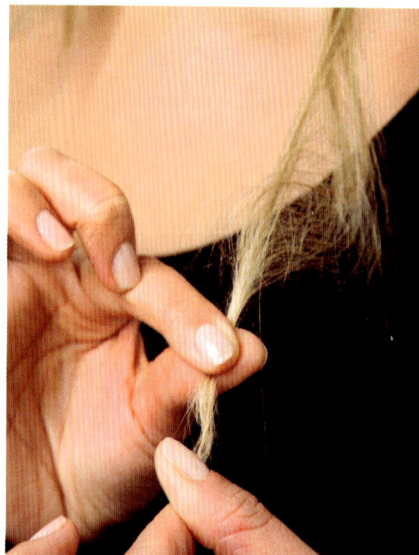

Pro Tips

- Get to know your waxes, putties and styling creams by rubbing them between your thumb and fingertip – the more fibrous they feel, the more texture they'll create.
- Using a shiny pomade or glossing cream to define a few ends can lend an overall impression of shine to a look that's actually quite matt and messy.
- To give a tight updo a soft-focus finish, hold your hands flat against the side of your head and rotate your palms and fingers in small circles over your scalp. This will lift up a few fine strands and create a delicately messy texture.

● step 2

Pick out a few random strands and twist the ends backwards and forwards between your fingers and thumb, to distribute the product and taper the tips.

step 3

To define longer strands, try rolling the mid-lengths and ends back and forth between your palms.

Straightening

Straightening is probably the fastest route to a well-groomed finish, whether you're creating a poker-straight style, tidying up your hairline before putting your hair up or smoothing down an unruly fringe. Straightening can also help prep thick or frizzy hair before curling, and is a great way to boost shine.

Pro Tools
- Sectioning clips
- Pintail or fine-tooth comb
- Straighteners
- Straightening serum or balm
- Heat-protective styling spray

Pro Techniques
- Sectioning

Pro Prep
- Smooth serum or straightening balm through wet or damp hair before blow-drying to a smooth finish, or mist heat-protective spray through clean, dry sections as below.

◑ step 1

Section your hair into two or three horizontal bands, depending on how thick or curly it is. Hair that's harder to style may need to be divided into more sections, so you can work on less hair at any one time.

➔ step 2

Mist the hair you're about to work on with a heat-protective styling spray.

Pro Tips

- Make sure your hair is totally dry before you start straightening, as exposing wet or damp hair to such high temperatures can cause damage and dehydration.
- For the best results, and to avoid going over the same section of hair more than once, wait till the plates of your straighteners are fully heated before you start. If your straighteners have a thermostat, 200ºC is hot enough to get the job done without causing unnecessary damage.
- To avoid creating kinks or burning your hair, move the straighteners all the way down each section without stopping.
- If you have thick or curly hair that's hard to tame, try ironing the roots a couple of times to encourage them to lie smoothly – your hair is stronger and younger here, so less prone to damage.
- Avoid over-straightening the tips, as these are older, weaker and more fragile than the roots and mid-lengths.
- Unless you have very thick hair or want a very flat finish, you may not need to straighten the roots of the layers underneath – but do straighten the roots of the top layers, for a smooth and shiny look from top to bottom.
- Create lift at the roots of your top layers by holding them up from your head at a greater angle as you pull the straighteners through.
- To help your hair hang in a natural curve, imagine you're guiding your straighteners round an imaginary balloon at the side of your head as you pull them through your hair, rotating your wrist slightly inwards as you work your way down.

⬆ step 3

Working on two-centimetre-wide sections of hair, and holding it at a slight angle away from the side of your head, move the comb down from root to tip, followed by the straighteners, in a slow, continuous movement.

⬆ step 4

When straightening your fringe, rotate your wrist slightly inwards as you move the plates down through the hair. This will curve the ends under and encourage your fringe to sit naturally.

⬆ step 5

Work your way through your hair from root to tip, letting it down section by section.

Curling with Tongs

Think way beyond ringlets – curling tongs can be used to create glamorous waves, disco-inspired curls or a casually tousled texture. Here's how to get started.

Pro Tools
- Pintail comb
- Natural bristle brush
- Heat-protective styling spray
- Curling tongs

Pro Techniques
- Sectioning

Pro Prep
- For the best results, always curl clean, dry, smoothly brushed or combed-through hair.
- If you have naturally thick, wavy or curly hair, blow-drying it straight before curling will give a smoother and more even finish.
- Sectioning your hair will make it easier to work with.

step 1

Take two-centimetre-wide sections of hair and prep with styling spray.

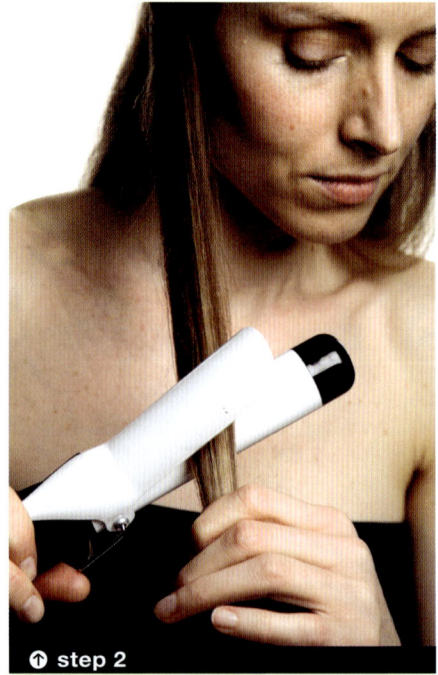

↑ step 2

Clamp the tongs around the end of the section. Ensure the ends of the hair are in the tongs smoothly to prevent any bends or kinks.

→ step 3

Wind the tongs up into the roots so the hair is sitting neatly and evenly along the barrel, rather than winding the hair over and over itself. This will help you heat the sections evenly from top to bottom.

→ step 4

Hold for between thirty seconds to a minute while your hair heats through – thick or curly hair (or a fatter section) will take longer to warm up.

Pro Tips

- For a polished look, brush each section before curling so the hair is smooth and straight.
- For a messier and more modern look, leave your ends and roots uncurled. Clamp the tongs onto your hair a few centimetres up from the tips, and stop winding when the tongs are a few centimetres away from your scalp.
- Curling a combination of wider and narrower sections will also give you a less formal effect. Or try tonging random sections in different directions, as well as leaving some sections uncurled.
- For an even more dishevelled look, try twisting each section from tip to root before wrapping it around the barrel of the tongs.
- To create larger, looser curls, use fatter tongs, or curl wider sections of hair.

↑ step 5

Unwind the curl by rotating the tongs out of the section in a downwards direction.

step 6

Mist with hairspray to hold, or style as required.

Pro Tip

If the clamp of your tongs are creating a kink in the ends of your hair, try holding the clamp open (or using clamp-free tongs) and using your fingers to carefully wind the section around and along the barrel. Hold the tongs a centimetre away from your scalp and wind from top to bottom of the section.

Curling with Rollers

A couple of strategically placed rollers can give your hair lift exactly
where it needs it most, while a full head can create all-over body and
bounce or make a blow-dry last much longer.

Pro Tools
- Natural bristle brush
- Rollers
- Hair dryer

Pro Techniques
- Blow-drying

Pro Prep
- For the best results, use
  your rollers after washing
  and blow-drying, while
  your hair is soft, warm
  and pliable.

step 1
Decide where your style
needs height or volume, and
whether you want to direct
your hair towards or away
from your face.

step 2
Take two-
centimetre
sections of hair
and blow-dry until
smooth and warm.

➔ step 3
Starting at the end of
each section, roll the hair
around the roller all the
way up to the roots,
where it will hold itself in
place against the scalp.
Use the fatter rollers
higher up on your head
for lift and volume, and
the smaller sizes around
your face, for a subtler lift
and a smaller curl.

↑ step 4

Once all your rollers are in position, spray with hairspray then leave to set for ten minutes. Alternatively, gently warm the hair with your dryer set to a low speed before allowing to cool.

Pro Tips

- Larger rollers will give more lift or volume, while smaller ones will create less lift and more of a curl.
- Because they're lighter, Velcro rollers (which we've used here) don't need to be pre-warmed, keep themselves in place without grips or clips, and are usually easier to use than the heavier, heated sets.
- Some rollers have ceramic strips inside. These retain more heat, so set the hair faster and give longer-lasting volume.
- Try preheating each section with straighteners rather than blow-drying, for an extra sleek effect.
- To curl the hair over rather than under the roller (best for creating volume and height), drape the ends of the hair over the roller before rolling it up into the roots.
- To roll in the opposite direction (best for directing your hair away from your face when you're working around your hairline), sit the roller on top of your ends rather than underneath them, then roll up into the roots. Play with size and placement for different effects – use smaller rollers to create more of a curl, or try curling your hair away from your face for a '70s flicked effect.

⊖ step 5

Carefully unwind the rollers and use your hands to guide the hair into position – or brush through to reduce some of the curl or height you've just created.

Chapter 4

BASIC STYLES

The techniques used in this chapter crop up again and again throughout the book, so it's worth taking the time to perfect them. You'll also end up with professional-looking versions of the plaits, ponytails and basic buns you wear every day.

Basic Ponytail

Clean and unfussy, if this style looks simple, that's because it is. But by taking the time to prep your hair, and throwing in a few finishing touches, you can take a classic ponytail a few steps away from its playground origins.

Pro Tools and Products
- Natural bristle brush
- Hair elastic or bungee band
- Styling cream
- Serum

⬆ step 1

Choose the position of your ponytail and brush your hair back into your hand.

⬆ step 2

Secure tightly with a hair elastic or bungee band.

Pro Tips

- Give your ponytail body, movement and hold by running mousse or thickening spray through towel-dried hair, and blow-drying until smooth.
- Add extra gloss and tame flyaway strands by misting the head of your natural bristle brush with a light-hold hairspray before you start styling.
- For a looser look with more volume around the crown, pull your hair back with your fingers rather than a brush.
- For a chic and simple style, wear your ponytail a few centimetres above the nape of your neck.
- For a sportier look, wear it right in the centre of the back of your head.
- For a high-fashion feel, wear it high on the top of your head and straighten the ends.
- To keep very thick hair in place, use a bungee band instead of a traditional hair elastic.
- Play with the finished look by pulling a few tendrils free at the front to frame your face, or sliding the fine end of a pintail comb between your hair and scalp at the crown and sides and wiggling it upwards to lift the hair away from your head and create some volume.
- Changing your parting can create a whole new look – try pulling your hair back from a deep side parting into a low ponytail, letting the hair cover your ears as you sweep it back.

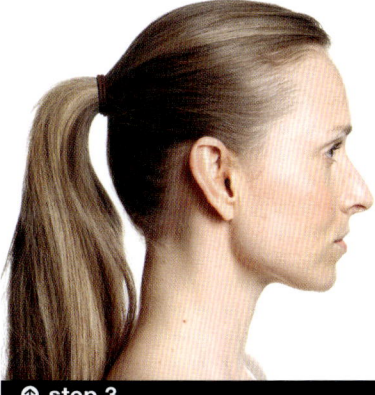

↑ step 3

Finish the look by smoothing a light styling cream or serum over the sides of your hair and through the lengths and ends of your ponytail.

The Half-Bun

Change the proportions of your ponytail by pulling it halfway through the band to create a looped bun.

⊙ step 1

Create your ponytail as usual, but stop twisting the hair elastic over the base when you get to the very last loop.

⊙ step 2

Pull the ponytail through the last loop of the elastic, but stop short of pulling it all the way through, to create a half-bun effect.

Pro Tip

Pull the hair further through to create a larger bun with a shorter tail, or try recreating the effect with a lower ponytail, or one that falls over one shoulder.

Basic Bun

The classic bun is one of the easiest techniques you'll ever learn – and once you've mastered the basics, you'll be able to create some of the more elaborate looks in this book, from a beautifully tousled topknot to a chic ballerina bun.

Pro Tools and Products
- Natural bristle brush
- Hair elastic or bungee band
- Kirby grips
- Medium-hold hairspray

⊕ step 1

Using a natural bristle brush, gather your hair at the nape of your neck.

⊕ step 2

Secure with a band to create a ponytail, then divide into two sections and pull to tighten.

⊕ step 3

Start coiling the ponytail around itself to create a bun shape, gently twisting as you go.

⊕ step 4

Secure your finished bun by pushing grips
firmly into the base, all the way around.

Product Tip

To hold your finished
look in place without
overloading it with product,
spray your hairspray on
to your hands and smooth
them gently over your hair.

Basic Plait

A schoolgirl staple, the basic plait comes into its own when you want a sleek and simple way to hold back your hair. It can be developed into more elaborate looks later on, such as French plaits and beach-inspired holiday plaits.

Pro Tools
- Natural bristle brush
- Hair elastic

➜ step 1

Securing prior to plaiting is optional, but it can help. Use an elastic to secure your hair into a low ponytail at the nape of your neck.

⬇ step 2

Split the ponytail into three equal widths. Start the plait by crossing one of the outer sections over into the middle position.

⬆ step 3

Now cross the outer section from the opposite side over the top of the section next to it, and into the middle.

⏷ step 4

Repeat on alternate sides all the way down to the bottom of your ponytail.

Product Tips

- Smooth flyaway strands by misting hairspray over your hands and running them over your plait.
- Finish off the tip with a dab of styling cream, for a soft shine and a prettily tapered shape.

⏶ step 5

Secure the end with an elastic.

Pro Tip

- Make the hair easier to handle by working with slightly damp hands.
- Prevent the end of your plait from looking lumpy by using smaller hair elastics, and choose neutral colours or clear elastics to give the look more of a grown-up feel.
- For a looser look, gather your hair back into a ponytail, but start plaiting straightaway instead of fastening with the first elastic.

Plaited Bun

Cross the perfect plait with a simple bun, to create a neat but pretty combination of the two.

Pro Tools and Products
- Natural bristle brush
- Hair elastics
- Kirby grips
- Firm-hold hairspray

⬇ step 1

To create a firmer base for your bun, start with a plait that you've fastened at each end.

⬆ step 2

Holding the base of the plait in place, start coiling the length of the plait around itself to create the bun.

⬆ step 3

Gently push a few long kirby grips through the base of your bun and into your scalp to hold the style in place. Finish with firm-hold hairspray.

Product Tip

Distribute a few drops of serum or dabs of styling cream on your palms and fingers, and smooth your hands over your hair for a sleek and glossy finish.

French Plait

The French plait is just a step away from the basic plaiting technique,
but the overall look is a far sleeker affair.

Pro Tools and Products
- Pintail comb
- Natural bristle brush
- Hair elastic
- Medium-hold hairspray

Pro Techniques
- Sectioning
- Basic plait

⬆ step 1

Separate off a half-moon section at the front of the
head and smooth it through with a natural bristle brush.

⬆ step 2

Divide the half-moon section into three equal pieces.

⬆ step 3

Begin to plait, crossing each section over the middle once only. Add extra hair into the outside section as you go.

➔ step 4

Then continue to plait and every time you take an outer section into the middle, pick up an extra piece from the side and incorporate it into the plait.

◉ **step 5**

Continue until the sides have all been incorporated and plaited all the way down to the end of your hair. Fasten with an elastic and spray to hold.

⬆ **step 6**

Break up the look by loosening the top with your fingers to create height and texture. You could also pull some tendrils free to frame your face.

Product Tip

For a slick finish, smooth a light styling cream over the sides.

Chapter **5**

OCCASION LOOKS

Now you know how to handle a range of basic techniques, it's time to put them all together and create some more elaborate looks – you'll also pick up a few tips and techniques that will help you personalise the final styles.

Pro Tools and Products
- Sectioning clips
- Pintail comb
- Curling tongs (a wand is used here)
- Natural bristle brush
- Mousse
- Thickening spray
- Firm-hold heat-protective hairspray
- Shine spray or lightweight styling cream

Pro Techniques
- Sectioning
- Curling with tongs
- Separating curls
- Backbrushing

Pro Prep
- Work a generous amount of mousse through the lengths and ends of freshly washed and towel-dried hair.
- Blow-dry using your hands rather than a brush, so the finished texture isn't too smooth.
- Apply thickening spray and dry again.
- Part your hair in the centre.

Red Carpet Curls

For an A-list look with va-va-voom, try soft and glossy waves. This style starts life as a full head of tight curls, but uses a backbrushing technique to break up the texture and create extra volume.

⬆ step 1

Section your hair horizontally from temple to temple, and curl two-centimetre-wide sections from root to tip, misting each section with a heat-protective firm-hold hairspray before curling.

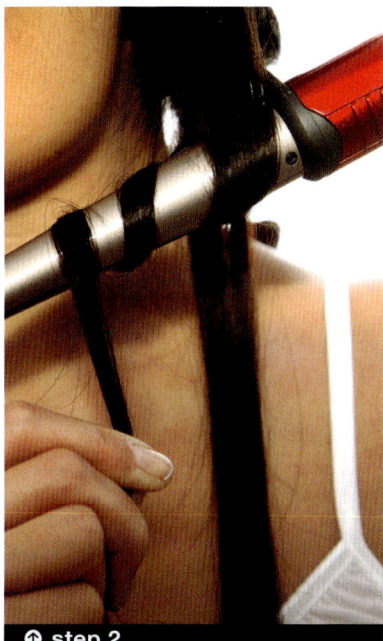

⬆ step 2

Hold the hair around the barrel of the tongs for between thirty and forty seconds. Release the freshly tonged section and pull it down as it cools, to stretch and lengthen the curl.

⬆ step 3

When the bottom section is fully curled, unclip the section above and continue tonging. Repeat until all hair is curled.

↩ step 4

Gently break up the curls with your fingers, pulling each one apart from top to bottom.

⬆ step 5

Create texture and volume by backbrushing from underneath with a natural bristle brush.

⬇ step 6

Mist with shine spray or use your fingers to gently run styling cream through the mid-lengths and ends.

Pro Tips

- Curl every section in the same direction, to give the waves a smooth and uniform look.
- Pulling the ringlets apart with your fingers and then brushing them out creates a soft and natural feel, and leaves the curls looking less 'set'. Avoid dragging your fingers through the curls, or they may lose their shape.

Product Tips

To add shine without weighing your curls down, look for an oil-free glossing spray or styling cream and avoid getting product too near your roots.

Pro Tools and Products
- Pintail comb
- Gel
- Medium-hold hairspray

Pro Techniques
- Creating partings

Pro Prep
- Smooth gel through freshly washed and towel-dried hair, or mist with a water spray until damp and then apply your gel.

Finger Waves

Inspired by the Hollywood waves of the 1920s, this is a soft and feminine way of styling and setting a shorter crop.

⬆ step 1

Part your hair to one side, using the fine end of your pintail comb.

step 2

Comb your hair straight on either side of the parting.

step 3

Working on the deeper side of the parting, comb your hair forwards in a diagonal direction for two centimetres. Stop combing and hold the hair in place with your fingers, just behind the comb.

⊙ step 4

Still holding the hair in place with your fingers, continue combing, but move the comb diagonally towards the back of your head. Hold in position after couple of centimetres, while still holding the first wave in place.

step 5

Continue combing all the way across, changing direction after every few centimetres and holding each new wave in place with a finger.

step 6

Blow-dry on a low speed setting, or leave to dry naturally. Spray with hairspray.

Pro Tips

- Make sure you comb all the way down to the scalp, to draw all your hair into the wave.
- Hold your comb so the teeth point down vertically towards the scalp rather than on a slant.

Pro Tools and Products
- Natural bristle brush
- Kirby grips
- Medium-barreled curling tongs
- Flat sectioning clips
- Lightweight mousse
- Light-hold heat-protective hairspray
- Serum or shine spray

Pro Techniques
- Basic blow-dry
- Curling with tongs

Pro Prep
- Work mousse through the lengths and ends of freshly washed and towel-dried hair.
- Blow-dry, apply thickening spray and dry again to a smooth finish with lift and volume at the roots.

Hollywood Waves

Setting large sections of carefully tonged hair helps to create a this sleek, silver-screen effect.

⬆ step 1

Mist the lengths and ends of your hair with a light-hold hairspray, then sweep it over one shoulder with a natural bristle brush.

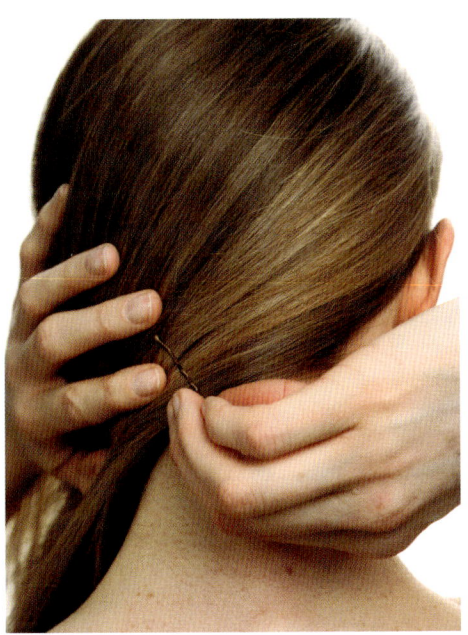

Pro Tip

Cross-pinning (pushing one kirby grip over another to form an 'X') helps hold a lot of hair in one place, and works well wherever you've created a lot of volume.

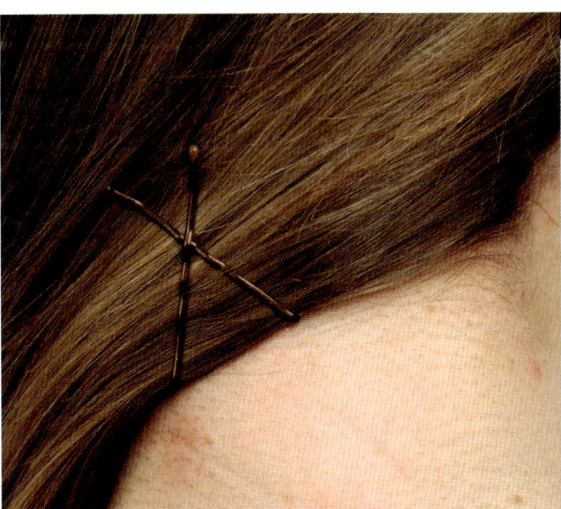

← step 2

Pulling the hair firmly round the back of your head, pin it into position at the nape of your neck. Push one grip over another for a really firm hold. Continue to add more kirby grips if needed, especially if you have thick hair.

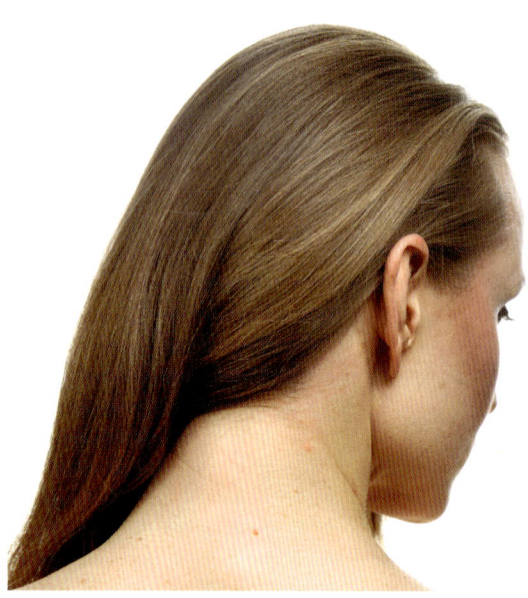

← step 3

Let your hair fall loosely over your opposite shoulder, concealing the kirby grips.

step 4

Section the hair at the temple, twisting and clipping the top section cleanly out of the way.

→ step 5

Mist sections of five to eight centimetres across with hairspray and tong from the bottom of each section, rolling the hair up towards the roots. Hold the tongs in position while the hair heats all the way through, then gently release and allow to cool. Repeat this process working up the hair, section by section until all the hair is curled.

⊙ step 6

Using a soft round brush, start brushing the hair out from top to bottom using long sweeping strokes until the hair starts to form soft waves.

Pro Tips

- To create an evenly waved effect, tong every section in the same direction.
- Clip the hair wherever the waves dip in towards the side of your head. Avoid creating kinks by placing a sheet of tissue paper between the clips and the hair.

step 8

Carefully remove the clips. Smooth a light serum carefully over the surface area of the hair and mist again with hairspray to hold.

⬆ step 7

To set the wave, hold the hair in place with flat sectioning clips, mist with hairspray and leave to set for ten minutes.

Pro Tools and Products
- Sectioning clips
- Slim-barrelled curling tongs
- Small silver sectioning pins
- Natural bristle brush or round brush
- Firm-hold mousse
- Heat-protective spray
- Serum, soft wax or styling cream
- Shine spray

Pro Techniques
- Horizontal sectioning
- Blow-drying
- Curling with tongs

Pro Prep
- Work a generous amount of mousse through washed and towel-dried hair, then blow-dry as smoothly as possible.
- Separate into two-centimetre horizontal sections.

Disco Curls

A simple setting technique followed by gentle backbrushing turns a headful of narrow ringlets into a cloud of soft and fluffy curls.

step 1

Working through the hair horizontally in two-centimetre sections, mist each section with a heat-protective hairspray and curl from tip to root, clamping the ends securely into the tongs, and winding all the way up.

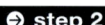 **step 2**

Hold the tongs in place for up to a minute, allowing the hair to heat all the way through.

Pro Tips
- Because the sections are so small and need to be curled from root to tip, it is easy to burn your fingers. Avoid this by using the clamp of the tongs and winding it up into the roots, instead of winding your hair around the tongs manually.
- For an evenly curled effect, curl every section in the same direction, making sure they're all the same size.

Product Tips

If you find your hair doesn't
hold the curls, apply a
second layer of mousse
or thickening spray after
blow-drying, and dry again.

➔ step 3

Release the curl, then carefully slide
it off the barrel and pin it against
your scalp before moving on to the
next section.

← step 4

When all the curls are
pinned into position,
mist all over with a
firm-hold hairspray
and leave to set for
about ten minutes.
When your hair feels
completely cool, start
unwinding the curls
in the order you
put them in.

⬆ step 5

Once all the curls have been unpinned, pull your fingers through your hair to break up the texture.

⬅ step 6

For a fluffier and voluminous finish, work through the hair with a natural bristle brush, brushing in short, downward strokes starting at the bottom and gradually moving up the hair shaft from tip to root. Then add volume by backbrushing from underneath.

step 7

Define the curls around your face with a dab of serum, soft wax or styling cream, then mist with hairspray to hold. Finish with shine spray so the curls catch the light.

Pro Tools and Products
- Pintail comb
- Straighteners
- Sectioning clips
- Hair dryer
- Paddle brush
- Heat-protective styling spray
- Shine serum
- Light-hold hairspray

Pro Techniques
- Sectioning
- Blow-drying
- Straightening

Pro Prep
- Smooth serum through wet hair.
- Blow-dry as smoothly as possible, using a paddle brush.
- Clip away a narrow D-section, starting and finishing at the outer end of both eyebrows.

Poker Straight

This expensively groomed look has a sleek and glassy finish with not a hair out of place.

⬆ step 1

Mist the area you'll be working on first with a heat-protective styling spray. This will help hold the look, and protect your hair from the high temperatures needed for a super-smooth texture.

⬆ step 2

Working with quite wide sections, follow the straightening tips on page 90 as you comb through the hair from mid-lengths to ends.

⬆ step 3

Keep the straighteners steady and work in a slow but sweeping motion, so you move from beginning to end without stopping, and pull through the tips of each section without altering the angle of the straighteners.

➡ step 4

When you reach the top section, straighten right from the roots, for extra smoothness and shine where it matters most.

⬆ step 5

When straightening your fringe, turn the straighteners slightly in and under when you reach the ends, to help the hair sit naturally.

⬆ step 6

Work a small amount of shine serum through your mid-lengths and ends.

⬆ step 7

Smooth whatever's left on your fingers lightly over the very top and mist with hairspray to hold.

Pro Tips

- If your hair is particularly fine, avoid straightening your roots when you reach the top section, or you will lose too much volume.
- If you have particularly thick or curly hair, you should be able to straighten each section from root to tip without losing much body.
- If your hair is hard to straighten, work with finer sections rather than ironing the same length again and again.
- Avoid overloading with hairspray (which can leave finer hair looking limp and flat) by spraying your fingers and running them over your mid-lengths and ends.

Pro Tools and Products
- Pintail comb
- Sectioning clips
- Straighteners
- Straightening balm
- Light-hold hairspray
- Shine spray

Pro Techniques
- Sectioning
- Straight blow-dry
- Straightening

Pro Prep
- Work straightening balm through freshly washed hair.
- Blow-dry as smoothly as possible.

Seventies Flicks

The flicked-out ends of this poker-straight look cascade all the way down to the shoulders, but would look just as good on a shorter style.

⬆ step 1

Section your hair horizontally from temple to temple and follow the basic straightening steps on page 90.

➔ step 2

Draw the straighteners smoothly down the hair shaft, but as you get closer to the end of each section, start curving the straighteners away from your face.

⬅ step 3

As you draw the straighteners out of the end of each section in an upwards direction, let the flicked-out tips fall into the palm of your hand and mist the ends with hairspray while they cool. When the hair is cool and the flick has set, gently release.

⬆ step 4

Repeat all the way round to the front sections. The closer you get to your face, the higher up the hair shaft you should start flicking your straighteners out, for a graduated effect.

step 5

Finish with shine spray for a polished and glossy effect.

Pro Tips

- Try pinning your flicks into your head while still warm misting with hairspray, and releasing when cool.
- For a more exaggerated flick, use your hair dryer on a low speed setting and gently elevate flicks while spraying hairspray into the air stream.

Product Tips

You can define and separate your flicks by using a soft wax or clay on the ends.

Pro Tools and Products
- Fine-tooth comb
- Styling clay, wax, paste or putty
- Lightweight hairspray or glossing spray

Pro Techniques
- Defining ends
- Creating partings

Pro Prep
- Blast freshly washed hair with a hair dryer on medium/high setting.

Textured Pixie Crop

Twisting the ends and creating a new parting can lend a short and choppy crop a whole new look. Play with products to experiment with texture, hold and shine.

⊕ step 1

Work your chosen styling product right into your roots by warming it up in your fingers and palms, then rubbing them from side to side through dry hair and over your scalp.

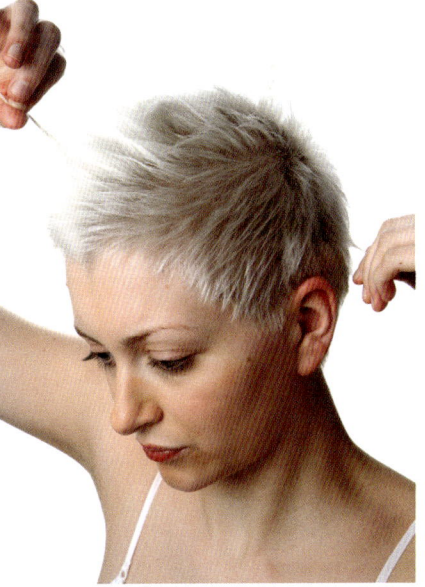

⬆ step 2

Create height by working your fingers up through your hair from root to tip.

Pro Tip

For a soft and feminine finish, make sure you define a few random strands around your face and at the nape of your neck.

➜ step 3

Using what's left on your fingertips, pick out random sections and twist between your fingers and thumb to define the ends.

⊕ step 4

For a sleeker look, use a fine-tooth comb to create a mini side sweep. Comb the front section into a side-swept fringe, leaving height and body at the back of the head.

⊕ step 5

Finish with a very light hairspray, or try a glossing spray for more shine.

Product Tips

- If you're finding it hard to get lift and volume into your hair, try using a volumising shampoo and skip the conditioner, which can weigh shorter styles down.
- Or try applying a lightweight volumising mousse to freshly washed and towel-dried hair, and then setting with your hair dryer on a slow speed and low heat.
- Avoid overloading fine hair with heavy styling products, and look for oil-free formulations.
- For medium hold, use a styling clay or soft wax; for a softer, shinier look, use a lightweight styling cream. To distribute evenly, rub into your hands until your fingers and palms are thinly coated with product.
- For a firmer finish with a pliable texture, use a fibrous styling paste or putty. Activate before using by rubbing it into your fingers and palms, then hold your hands together, pressing and releasing until you see the fibres forming like fine strands of elastic.

Pro Tools and Products
- Hair dryer
- Sectioning clip
- Natural bristle brush
- Curling tongs
- Paddle brush
- Mousse
- Thickening spray
- Light clay, wax or styling cream
- Light-hold hairspray

Pro Techniques
- Rough drying
- Curling with tongs
- Finger-teasing
- Backbrushing
- Defining ends

Pro Prep
- Work a generous amount of mousse through the lengths and ends of freshly washed and towel-dried hair.
- Blow-dry using your hands rather than a brush, so the finished texture isn't too smooth.
- Apply thickening spray and dry again.

Tousled Bed Head

Curling, backbrushing and finger-teasing help create this deliberately rumpled, rock 'n' roll look.

⬆ step 1

Section your hair horizontally from ear to ear and clip the top half into a loose twist. Curl randomly chosen sections from bottom to top, leaving the tips free of the tongs.

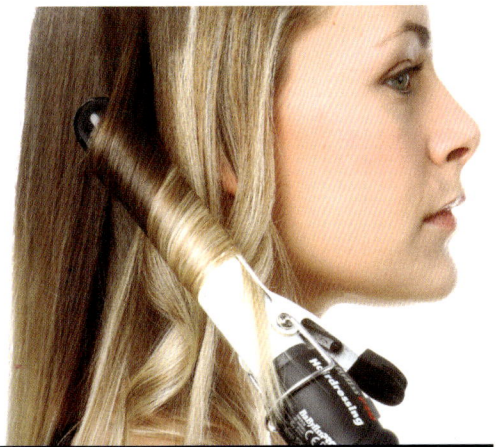

⬆ step 2

Let another layer down by unclipping your hair and re-sectioning from temple to temple. Curl your way randomly through the hair you've just released.

⬆ step 3

Unclip the remaining section and continue curling random pieces until you've curled most (but not all) of your hair.

⬆ step 4

Break up the curls by brushing them out with a paddle brush. This will turn them into a looser kink, and create a tousled rather than curled look.

↑ step 5

Finger-tease a few tendrils here and there. To do this, hold onto the tip of the hair while sliding your fingers gently up the shaft, working half to three-quarters of the way up into the hair. Backbrush from underneath for extra volume and texture if needed.

Product Tips

- Use a generous amount of mousse or thickening spray to give your hair the 'bite' it needs to hold this look – especially if it's freshly washed, or is naturally soft, fine and shiny.
- Keep products away from your roots to avoid weighing your hair down. A final blast of dry shampoo at the roots is the only exception. This can create a matt and messy texture without dragging your hair down.

Pro Tips

- To avoid smoothing your hair down too much before you start, use your hands to help you blow your hair dry, rather than a brush.
- For a naturally haphazard effect, wind some pieces one way around the barrel of the tongs and others in the opposite direction.
- Leave the hair flatter at the roots by winding your tongs halfway up the hair shaft, stopping when they're a few centimetres away from your scalp.
- To keep the volume of this look in check, aim to tong about half to three-quarters of your hair, leaving some sections uncurled.

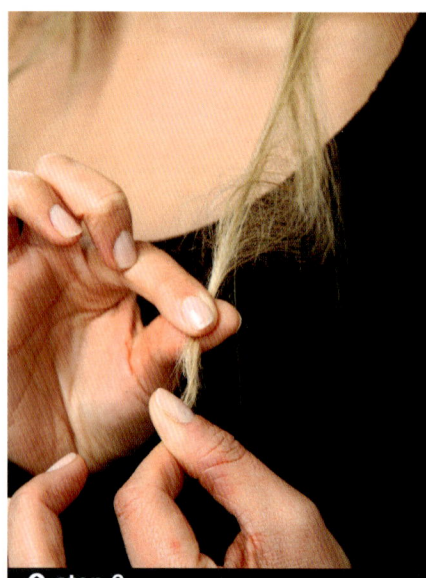

↑ step 6

Add shine and definition by twisting a light styling clay, wax or soft cream through some random ends. Mist the finished look lightly with hairspray.

Pro Tools and Products
- Hair elastic or bungee band
- Kirby grips
- Serum or light styling cream
- Light- to medium-hold hairspray

Pro Techniques
- Basic ponytail
- Basic bun
- Finishing ends

Pro Prep
- Work mousse through damp or dry hair.
- Blow-dry, using your hands if your hair is fine or silky.
- If your hair is prone to frizzing, smooth it with a natural bristle brush as you blow-dry.

Tousled Bun

The wavy texture of this romantic-looking bun helps hold the hair in place, making it much easier to style than it might look.

⬆ step 1

Gather your hair into a loose, low ponytail over one shoulder.

→ step 2

Rotate the outside of the hair inwards then fasten your hair loosely at the nape of the neck with a hair elastic or bungee band.

Pro Tip

If your hair is naturally straight, try creating some texture by following the tonging techniques described on page 92, either curling your hair from a few centimetres below the roots or just tonging the ponytail in two-centimetre wide sections after fastening at the nape of the neck. Brush through after tonging to break up the curls, using a natural bristle brush.

⬆ step 3

Twisting your ponytail slightly as you wind it round its own base, begin to coil it into a bun.

Pro Tip

Wiggle your grips through the hair in a weaving motion as you push them into the base of the bun. This will anchor them well into the hair and keep the bun firmly in place.

⬆ step 4

Continue winding until you reach the end of the ponytail. Secure the finished bun by pinning kirby grips into its base, trying not to flatten it out of shape as you push the grips in.

← **step 5**

Pull a few tendrils free from the bun and others from around your face to soften the look and add a romantic feel. Define the ends with serum or styling cream.

Product Tips

- Working a small amount of serum or styling cream through your hair before pulling it back into a ponytail will give it a subtle shine without knocking out its natural texture.
- This style works beautifully on naturally wavy hair. Enhance your curls by using a curl-defining cream or scrunching mousse into damp hair.
- For fine or straight hair use a generous amount of mousse before curling with small- or medium-barrelled tongs.

➜ step 6

Mist with hairspray to hold. Try adding an accessory to personalise your style and add a touch of glamour.

Pro Tips

- Because bungee bands give you more control over the tightness of a ponytail than traditional bands do, they're particularly helpful here, as the hair should be held firmly in place but not pulled too tightly.
- To use a bungee band, hook one end into the base of your ponytail and wrap it round and round, holding it taut until you reach the end of the band. Then hook it back into the underside of your ponytail.

Pro Tools and Products

- Pintail comb
- Sectioning clips
- Natural bristle brush
- Kirby grips
- Medium- or large-barrelled curling tongs
- Mousse or thickening spray
- Medium-hold hairspray

Pro Techniques

- Sectioning
- Backbrushing
- Curling with tongs
- Finger-teasing

Pro Prep

- Work mousse or thickening spray through towel-dried hair, then blow-dry with a natural bristle brush.
- Create a deep D-section with a pintail comb.

Modern Bardot

While backbrushing the crown gives this look its retro appeal, the bed-headed texture and tousled tendrils make it a modern-day classic.

⬆ step 1

Gathering the sectioned-off hair into one hand, hold it gently but firmly forwards and backbrush from the mid-lengths down into the roots with sweeping strokes.

⬆ step 2

Work your way forwards through the section using long sweeping movements brushing away from the head until it's been fully backbrushed (you'll eventually have no hair left in your hand).

⬆ step 4

Once you're happy with the shape, gather the hair at the back of your head, just below the crown, and get ready to pin into position.

⬆ step 3

Gently brush the hair back over your head, smoothing over the top layer without flattening the volume underneath.

Pro Tip

Cross-pinning is often used to hold a lot of hair in position, without pulling it too tightly or flattening the volume you've worked hard to create. Push one grip into the hair and along the scalp. Push another diagonally through the first to create an 'X'.

⊙ step 5

For a prettily rolled effect, twist the hair slightly, then use a cross-pinning technique to hold it firmly in place.

⊙ step 6

Curl wide sections of hair around medium- or large-barrelled curling tongs, to create four or five large ringlets.

Pro Tips

- Backbrushing won't hold on silky-soft hair, so don't try to blow-dry too smoothly when you're preparing for this style. Better still, wash and dry your hair the day or night before you style it.
- Curl your hair in random directions, to create a softer and less formal look.
- Create a fluffier texture by backbrushing the curls from underneath and finger-teasing some random tendrils.
- Finally, frame your face by pulling a few strands free from the top section and finger-teasing them for texture and volume.

step 7

To turn the curls into a looser wave, brush them through with a natural bristle brush. Mist with hairspray to hold.

Pro Tools and Products
- Natural bristle brush
- Hair elastic or bungee band
- Kirby grips
- Light-hold gel
- Serum or straightening balm
- Hairspray

Pro Techniques
- Basic ponytail

Pro Prep
- Smooth serum or straightening balm through damp hair before blow-drying to a smooth, straight finish.

Low Slung Ponytail

This sleek and simple ponytail is the ultimate in easy chic. Wrapping a section of hair neatly around the base of the tail is a small touch with big impact.

⏷ step 1

Mist the head of a natural bristle brush with hairspray and use it to smooth your hair into a low ponytail over one shoulder.

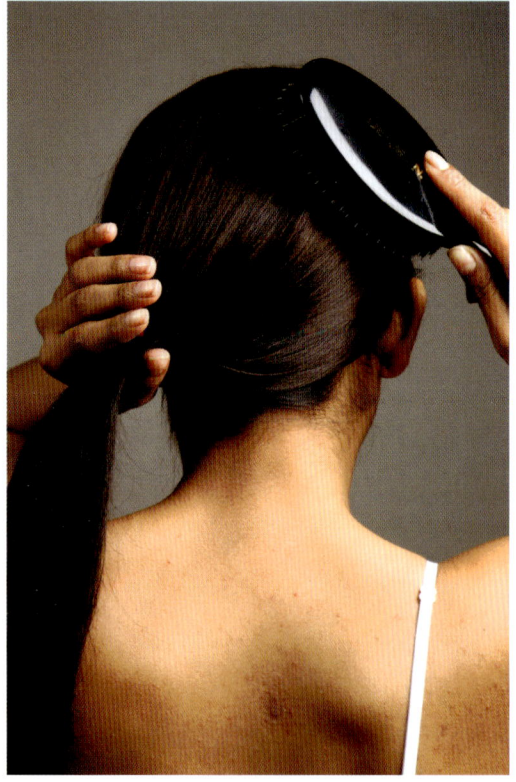

↑ step 2

Fasten securely with a hair elastic or bungee band. If you have thick hair, a bungee will keep it firmly in position without pulling it too tightly and creating kinks or creases in the hair.

↑ step 3

Take a narrow section of hair from the base of the ponytail and wind it over the top of the elastic or bungee.

⬆ step 4

Use a kirby grip to fasten the end of the section underneath the base of the ponytail.

Product Tips

If the section you're winding around the base of your ponytail keeps escaping from its grip, keep it in place by coating it with a lightweight gel, or use your fingers to smooth hairspray from top to bottom first.

Pro Tip

To fix a bungee band firmly into position, hook one end into the underside of the ponytail, pull up firmly and wrap it around the hair until you reach the end, then hook it back into the hair.

step 5

Run a small amount of serum over the surface layer of the hair and pony, then mist with hairspray to hold.

Pro Tools and Products
- Paddle brush
- Hair dryer
- Fine-tooth comb
- Mini straighteners
- Natural bristle brush
- Hair elastic or bungee band
- Kirby grips
- Light-hold hairspray
- Serum
- Styling cream

Pro Techniques
- Straight blow-dry
- Straightening
- Basic ponytail

Pro Prep
- Work serum through wet hair before towelling off and blow-drying.

Catwalk Ponytail

A sleek texture and poker-straight tail gives this look a sculpted feel, while concealing the band with a slim section of hair adds to the groomed and grown-up finish.

⬆ step 1

Following the steps on page 79, blow-dry your hair with a paddle brush for a straight, smooth finish.

⬆ step 2

Straighten the hair along your hairline, starting from your fringe, working around the ears and down to the nape of your neck.

⬆ step 3

Spritz your brush with hairspray and brush your hair firmly up into the palm of your hand. Continue adding hairspray if needed and brush until smooth.

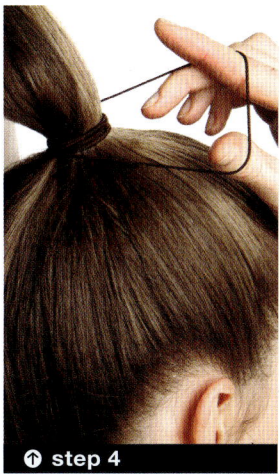

⬆ step 4

Fasten into a high ponytail with an elastic or bungee. Bungees may be better for this style to prevent kinks or dents in the hair.

⬅ step 5

Take a thin section of hair and wind it neatly around the base of your ponytail, concealing the band underneath.

Product Tips

- Using a natural bristle brush to create your ponytail will give your hair a smooth and shiny finish.
- To tame static and flyaway strands, spray the bristles of the brush with hairspray first.
- Add a final touch of gloss by smoothing over the finished look with a dab of serum worked into your palms and fingers, or mist with shine spray.

Pro Tip

Try tipping your head back as you gather your hair to create your high ponytail, and hold the hair taut to stop it from looking loose and baggy at the base, while brushing the hair into your hand, secure with a bungee. Comb any lumps or bumps in towards the base of the pony, misting with hairspray as you go, to hold. Remove the bungee (hair should stay in position now) and gently smooth out those imperfections before resecuring.

⬆ step 6

Pin in position under the base of the ponytail and let the ponytail fall down to cover the join.

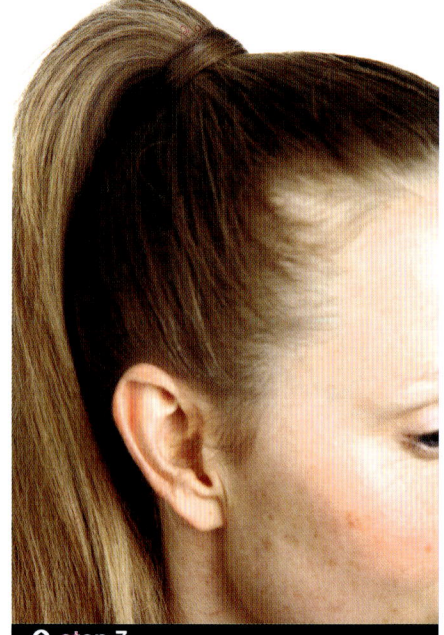

⬆ step 7

Mist light-hold hairspray over your palms and fingers and smooth down any frizzy areas.

Pro Tools
- Hair elastic

Pro Techniques
- Basic plait
- Finishing ends

Pro Prep
- Work mousse through the mid-lengths and ends of towel-dried hair. Leave to dry naturally, or dry with a diffuser to bring out a natural wave.

Beach Plait

This holiday-friendly plait works well when your hair is thickened by sea salt and wind-whipped into a tousled texture, but looks just as good on naturally wavy hair types.

⬆ step 1

Divide your hair into three equal sections as if you were going to create a classic plait at the nape of your neck, but pull them gently off-centre as you start to plait them together.

⊖ step 2

As you work your way down the hair, direct your plait over one shoulder and continue plaiting all the way to the end.

Pro Tip

Pulling your hair forwards over your shoulder before starting to plait helps the finished plait to curve naturally around your neck, and prevents a bump from forming at the back of your head.

➜ step 3

Fasten the ends with an elastic. Loosen up the look and fatten the plait by gently teasing out a few random sections, without pulling them completely free from the plait.

Pro Tips

- For a playful holiday look, secure one end of a ribbon at the base of the plait with a kirby grip and incorporate it into one of the sections as you braid your way down the hair. Once you've fastened the end of the plait, wind the ribbon over the elastic and tuck the end underneath, not forgetting to remove the kirby grip from the top and wind any excess ribbon around and secure with a grip.
- To prep naturally straight hair for this look, apply mousse after washing and towel drying, then rough dry. Follow the tonging instructions on pages 92–95 to curl your hair in two-centimetre sections, ending the curls eight to ten centimetres away from the roots. Brush out the curls with a natural bristle brush to create a soft wave, spritz with sea salt spray and plait as above.
- If you're recreating this look on holiday, mix a small amount of sunscreen with a leave-in conditioner and run it through damp hair before creating your plait. Leave it to dry naturally before teasing out a few pieces. This will create texture, tame flyaways and protect your hair from the sun.
- Feel free to style and define sections around the face, add a fringe or a quiff, and set with hairspray prior to starting your braid.

Pro Tools and Products
- Pintail comb
- Hair elastic
- Kirby grips
- Soft wax or styling cream
- Light- to medium-hold hairspray
- Sectioning clips

Pro Techniques
- Sectioning
- French plait
- Finishing ends

Pro Prep
- If you're working with freshly washed hair or very fine hair, smooth mouse or thickening spray through before blow-drying.

Halo Plait

This pretty plait winds its way around the head, and has a deliberately dishevelled texture that stops the finished style from looking too prim.

⬆ **step 1**

Use the pintail comb to create a vertical line running from just behind your ear to the very top of your head. Clip up all the hair in front of the divide with sectioning clips as you will use this later.

⬆ step 2

Take a wide section of hair from just behind your ear, divide into three equal parts and start plaiting them together using the French plaiting technique (see pages 110–113).

Pro Tip

To create a plait with a raised rather than flat look, divide hair into three equal parts as before, then carry the outer sections under rather than over the middle one as you plait your hair, as if you were plaiting upside down.

⬆ step 3

Continue using your French technique to create a plait that travels around your head at about two centimetres away from your hairline, adding hair from above and below as you go.

⬆ step 4

Continue to plait over the top of your head, unclipping the front section so you can incorporate it into the plait.

↑ step 5

When you return to your starting point behind the ear, all the hair has been gathered up into the plait. Continue working right down to the end, plaiting away from the head. Fasten with a fine elastic.

Pro Tips

- Don't worry if a few strands escape along the way — this style is meant to look a little messy, and you tidy up any lumps and bumps at the end by securing with kirby grips.
- The more tension you maintain while plaiting, the neater your halo plait will be.

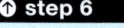

⬆ step 6

Tuck the loose end of the plait neatly into the base and pin to hold.

⬅ step 7

Finish the look by pulling out a few loose tendrils and pinning away any others that may look too messy. Twist the ends with a soft wax or styling cream to define. Spray to hold.

Pro Tools and Products
- Paddle brush
- Natural bristle brush
- Hair dryer
- Mini straighteners
- Hair elastic or bungee band
- Fine-tooth comb
- Kirby grips
- Light- to medium-hold hairspray

Pro Techniques
- Straight blow-dry
- Straightening
- Backcombing
- Basic bun
- Finger-teasing
- Finishing ends

Pro Prep
- Run a small amount of texturising or thickening spray through the hair prior to drying to add volume and texture.
- For coarse or frizzy hair apply a smoothing serum on to damp hair.

Ballerina Bun

This simple twisting technique turns a sleek ponytail into a super-sized topknot, while the soft-focus texture and loosened ends create a prettily undone look.

⊕ step 1

Follow the steps on pages 76–77, and blow-dry with a paddle brush, for a smooth, sleek finish.

Pro Tip

For a demure alternative, try prepping your hair with salt spray and blasting it dry before you begin. Then create a soft centre parting with your fingers, and position the bun a few centimetres above the nape of your neck, instead of high on the top of your head.

↑ step 2

Straighten the hair along your hairline, working your way from your fringe, around your ears and along the nape of your neck. This will help to create a groomed finish.

⊙ step 3

Using a natural bristle brush misted with a light-hold hairspray, brush your hair up into the palm of your hand and fasten into a high ponytail with an elastic or bungee.

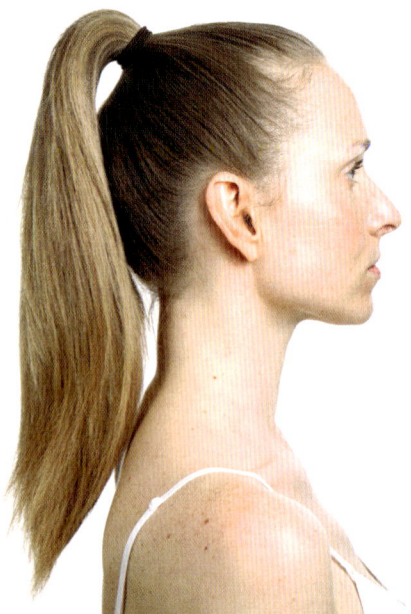

⊕ step 4

Firmly holding the ponytail above your head, gently twist the tail until it forms a thick rope.

⊕ step 5

Pull a few pieces free (but not totally loose) to dishevel the ponytail and create a messier texture with more volume. If you want to add more volume, use a comb or brush to backcomb from behind, working on the bottom few centimetres just above the base.

Pro Tip

If you find the overall look too severe for your face shape or want to soften the style, try gently raking your hair back with your fingers to create your ponytail, instead of smoothing it up with a brush. Finish by gently pulling some tendrils free around the face and hairline, and finger-teasing the ends to frame your face.

⬆ step 6

Coil the twisted ponytail around its own base to create a bun, pinning as you wrap, until it feels secure.

➔ step 7

Finish with your fingers, pulling more strands free and pinning others back into the bun to create a deliberately dishevelled effect. Mist with hairspray to hold.

Pro Tools and Products

- Pintail comb
- Sectioning clips
- Natural bristle brush
- Kirby grips
- Firm-hold hairspray
- Serum
- Styling cream

Pro Techniques

- Sectioning
- Defining ends

Pro Prep

- This style works best one or two days after washing, as clean hair can be too slippery and will need more styling product to create enough grip.

French Pleat

The height at the back and the softened texture around the face give this ladylike updo a modern twist.

step 1

Twist the top of your hair into a shallow D-section and clip it out of the way. Brush the rest back into the nape of your neck, as if you were creating a low ponytail.

⬆ **step 2**

Hold the fine end of the pintail comb vertically against one side of the hair, keeping it pressed firmly into the nape of the neck prior to twisting.

➔ step 3

Holding your hair firmly throughout, twist your hair upwards and begin wrapping it around the end of the comb, to create a pleat against the back of your head.

⊕ step 4

Maintain tension while holding the tail end of your hair out of the way, and pin the pleat in place, working all the way up the seam. Leave the comb in position for now.

step 5

Slide the comb out of the pleat, taking care not to snag or tangle any hair in the comb. Let the tail hang free.

step 6

Twist and tuck the tail end of the hair into the centre of the pleat, pinning firmly in place.

step 7

Unclip the D-section from the top of your head and brush it gently back over the top of the pleat.

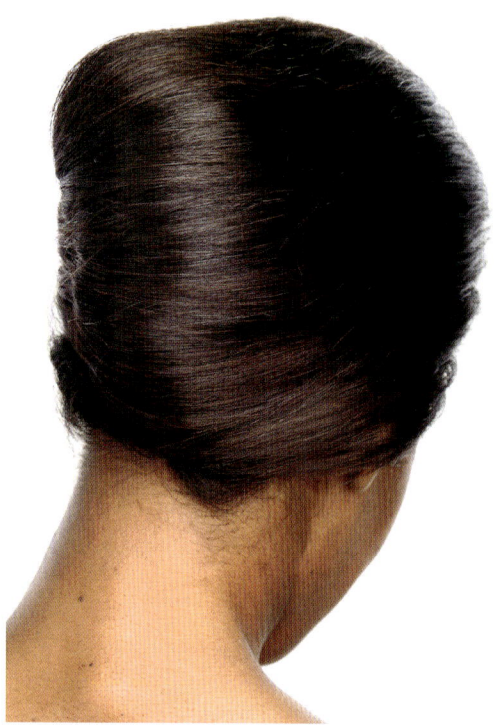

⊙ step 8

Wrap the hair over the top of the pleat, smoothing it down with the brush and pinning it carefully into the seam of the pleat.

step 9

For a classic formal finish, smooth down the sides with a dab of serum or smoothing cream, and mist with hairspray to hold. For a modern alternative, pull a few strands free, define the ends with a soft wax, serum or styling cream, and then mist with hairspray.

Pro Tips

- Always start this style with smooth hair – brush well with a natural bristle brush before you begin, and texturise the look later if you want a dishevelled effect.
- For more height at the front and top, backbrush the underneath of the D-section before you smooth it back over the pleat.
- Accentuate the height at the back of this look by adding a couple of thin headbands over the front and sliding them back into the style to create lift and volume at the crown.

Product Tips

To distribute the hairspray lightly and evenly over the surface of your hair, spray it onto your palms and fingers and smooth your hands over the finished look.

Pro Tools and Products
- Pintail comb
- Hair dryer
- Gel
- Firm-hold hairspray

Pro Techniques
- Creating partings

Pro Prep
- Start with freshly washed hair or mist with water until damp.

Smooth and Sleek

This low-maintenance, high-impact look will stay put all day.

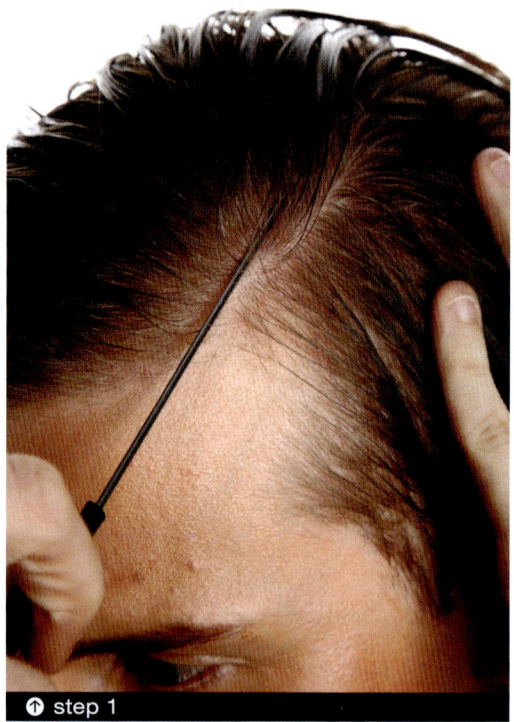

⬆ step 1

Section your hair into a side parting with the fine end of a pintail comb.

⬇ step 2

Smooth a generous amount of gel through the sides, working from the parting right down to the ends.

Product Tip

Shorter hair can be harder to control, so may need a gel with a firmer hold applied in smaller sections. Alternatively, try mixing equal parts of firm-hold gel and mousse together.

⬆ step 3

Comb carefully from root to tip to distribute the gel evenly through your hair, smoothing with your hands as you go.

➜ step 4

Set your dryer on a low speed and begin to dry, making sure you let your parting set first before moving down the sides and along to the ends.

⬅ step 5

Smooth the sides down with your palms and fingers, mist with hairspray and smooth again.

Pro Tips

- To set the style sooner, dry your roots well before moving onto the lengths and ends, keeping the dryer on a low speed to avoid dislodging your parting.
- Move your dryer gently from side to side all the way along your parting, keeping the nozzle a few centimetres away from your scalp.
- This style has a deliberately set look, so continue misting with hairspray and smoothing down with your hands until you feel your hair is held firmly in place and all flyaways have been tamed.

Pro Tools and Products
- Natural bristle brush
- Fine-tooth comb
- Firm-hold hairspray

Pro Techniques
- Backcombing

Pro Prep
- Spray generously with firm-hold hairspray.

The Quiff

An iconic rockabilly style, created with a bit of backcombing at the top and slicked-back sides.

⊙ step 1

Brush the side sections back with a natural bristle brush – as well as smoothing the hair into position, this will also distribute the hairspray through the lengths and ends.

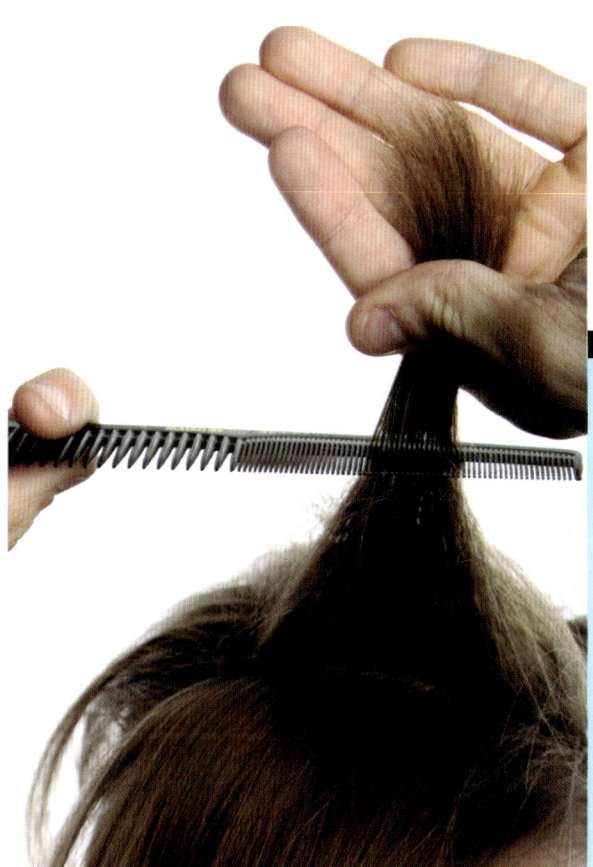

Pro Tip

The less hair you backcomb at a time, the more volume you'll create.

⊖ step 2

Section the hair by creating a deep fringe with the fine end of a pintail comb and pushing the hair forwards. Backcomb the top section working from the back to front. Gradually increase the amount of backcombing as you go.

⬇ step 3

Smooth the backcombed section back into position with the brush, being careful not to disturb the volume underneath.

Pro Tips

- You can smooth the sides into position with a comb instead of a brush, but the brush will give a sleeker, smoother finish.
- To create volume at the roots rather than the tips, start backcombing a couple of centimetres above your scalp, pushing the comb down in short, even strokes.
- Always backcomb the underside of your hair, so the surface looks smooth and shiny when you brush it back over the top.

step 4

Give the look a rougher edge by loosening and dishevelling pieces from the quiff with your fingers. Mist with firm-hold hairspray to hold.

Pro Tools and Products
- Hair dryer
- Mini straighteners
- Fine-tooth comb
- Light-hold hairspray
- Light wax or styling cream

Pro Techniques
- Basic rough dry
- Sectioning
- Straightening
- Finishing ends

Pro Prep
- Work mousse through damp hair for volume and control, or use salt spray for a beachy texture and volume.
- Dry shampoo will work wonders on one to two-day-old hair and gives a matt texture.

Short Preppy

This look combines straightening and texturising techniques to groom shorter styles, keeping them looking natural and touchable.

⬆ step 1

Directing the air into the roots, use your fingers to rough dry the top section.

➔ step 2

To build volume and texture at the back, lift the hair in a scrunching movement and point the dryer into the roots. Now remove the dryer, and hold the hair in place until it cools.

⊙ step 3

Tuck the hair back behind the ears, pull out small sections one at a time around the hairline, and smooth down with the mini straighteners.

⊙ step 4

Continue straightening the hairline, paying special attention to the sections around your ears and along the back of your hairline, and the nape of your neck.

Product Tip

Play with your finished look by changing your styling products. The softer a product feels when you run it between your finger and thumb, the softer your finished style will look. The drier the product feels, the stiffer your style.

⬆ step 5

Comb the front sections forward, following the comb with the straighteners for a smooth finish.

Pro Tips

• To straighten short hair without burning your fingers, use your comb to pick up the sections, comb towards the tip, and follow with your straighteners.

• The closer to the roots you take your straighteners, the more smooth and sleek your overall style will look.

• For a professionally groomed finish, spend more time straightening the hair around and behind your ears, as this can feel rough and look unruly.

• Personalise your look by defining the ends, smoothing down the front or tucking the sides behind your ears.

⬆ step 6

Twist a soft wax or styling cream into a few random ends for definition and malleability. Sweep the fringe into position and mist with light-hold hairspray.

Chapter 6

ADVANCED TECHNIQUES

This chapter will move your skills even further on by introducing you to a few trickier techniques, such as temporary extensions and trimming a fringe.

Pro Tools
- Pintail comb
- Sectioning clips
- Hair scissors

Pro Techniques
- Sectioning

Trimming a Fringe

A fringe can flatter your face shape, update a look you've grown bored of and even make fine hair seem thicker. Here's how to keep yours in trim, or if you're feeling reckless, how to create one from scratch.

⬆ step 1

Using the pintail comb, create a half-moon section and pin the hair on either side of your face behind your ears.

⬇ step 3

Holding your hair away from your face with the comb, and pointing the tips of the scissors diagonally up rather than horizontally across, cut small triangles into the ends of the hair, all the way across.

⬆ step 2

Comb from above and then from underneath, making sure the hair is lying as flat and straight as possible. Use straighteners to ensure an even finish.

⬆ step 4

Working in the same direction you followed in step 3, cut a second row of small triangles into the ends, but this time removing the points you created previously, working all the way across.

⬆ step 5

Work your way across the bottom of the fringe for a third time, by now you should have a straight line. This time snip away any loose or stray ends keeping your scissors on the diagonal.

◔ **step 6**

Holding your scissors vertically, slice delicately up into the fringe to remove fine slivers of hair – this will take away excess weight and soften up the effect.

Pro Tips

- For the most flattering effect, your half-moon section (which will determine the width of your finished fringe) should start and finish at the tail end of each eyebrow.
- The deeper the half-moon, the thicker your finished fringe will be, so the thicker you want them to look, the further back the curve should go.
- If you're cutting a very deep fringe, work your way back through the sectioned-off hair a bit at a time, letting it down in layers and taking care to cut each layer to the same length.
- Never trim a fringe without creating the 'zigzag' effect first. If you cut horizontally across on your first attempt, the scissors will push the hair to one side as you cut it and the finished fringe will look lopsided.
- Always cut your fringe when your hair is clean and dry. Hair is longer when it's wet, so a fringe that is cut into wet or damp hair could dry to a far shorter length than you intended.
- To make your hair much easier to cut, try blow-drying it smooth, or even straightening it before you start to cut.
- As well as creating a smooth, straight surface to work with, holding your hair with a comb (rather than with your fingers) means you won't pull it too tightly while you cut your fringe. Pulling the hair down or out will lengthen it artificially, so your fringe could end up shorter than you'd meant it to be.
- The higher you elevate your hair from your face while you cut your fringe, the more layered it will look, while the closer to your face you hold it, the blunter it will be. For a standard effect, hold the hair about five centimetres away from your face.
- Working your way across with the scissors held vertically gives a feathered finish that helps your fringe sit softly. The deeper you cut into your fringe, the softer and more obvious the feathering will look, so start with shallow snips and go deeper only if you need to.

Pro Tools
- Pintail comb
- Sectioning clips
- Hair extensions and clip attachments
- Hairspray

Pro Techniques
- Sectioning
- Backcombing

Using Hair Extensions

A few temporary extensions can make your hair seem longer and fuller, give it a natural-looking swing and are far easier to apply than you might think.

⬆ step 1

Section your hair so that you can get your extensions right into your roots and will have a layer of hair to let down over the clips after you've attached them.

⬇ step 2

Backcomb your hair at the roots. Mist the backcombed areas with hairspray. This will give the clips something to grip onto, especially if your hair is very soft or fine, or has just been washed.

⬆ step 3

Gently brush the extensions from root to tip, to straighten and untangle the strands.

⬇ step 4

Squeeze the clips to open up the jaws, manoeuvre them into position around the roots of the hair and release the clips to clamp them shut.

Where to Attach Your Extensions

- You can insert extensions wherever you want extra volume and fullness. Create as many tiers as you need.
- Always position your extensions symmetrically around your head, so the final effect looks even and natural.
- Clip your extensions into the roots about four centimetres away from your hairline, so they're further away from the surface of your hair, and less likely to be seen.

⬆ step 5

Cover up the clips by releasing the section of hair just above the extensions.

Pro Tips

- Increasing fullness is far easier than trying to lengthen the look of your hair, which would need many more extensions and can be harder to achieve in a way that looks natural.
- Extensions made from real hair will always look more natural than those made of synthetic fibres.
- Match your extensions as closely as possible to your natural hair colour.
- Extensions will rarely come in the same length as your own hair, so ask your stylist to trim them to fit.
- Treat extensions as you would treat your own hair. Wash, condition and dry them after every few wears, or they'll soon look dirty and can start to frizz.
- If you'll be using extensions regularly, invest in a tangle teezer – a detangling tool that gently undoes knotted strands without damaging them.
- If your final style will be straightened or tonged, use the same techniques to straighten or curl your extensions before clipping them in.

Putting Your Own Extensions Together

Extensions with the clips already attached can make your job much easier, but can also be more expensive, so many professional stylists sew on the clips themselves. Most extensions will need a clip sewn onto either end of the base, but if it's wider than eight-to-ten centimetres, sew a clip into the middle as well, for an extra-firm hold.

Chapter 7

COLOUR

The right colour can make your hair look thicker, shinier and healthier, and your skin and eyes seem brighter. This chapter will guide you through the process of choosing and applying a home colour kit, and tell you what's available in the salon too.

COLOUR AT HOME

Colouring your hair at home is quicker and cheaper than visiting the salon – and doesn't have to end in disaster, as long as you aim for a subtle change rather than a whole new hue, and follow the instructions in the box. Choosing a new colour becomes much easier once you understand which shades will flatter your skin tone most.

Choosing Your Hue

Facing a wall-to-wall display of colouring kits can be baffling at best. Here's how to navigate your way through what's available…

step 1

Before you think about colour, narrow the field by asking yourself a few simple questions. Do you want to cover grey or just add shine? Do you want an all-over colour or to touch up your highlights, lowlights or just your roots? And do you want a colour that will fade gradually or one that you'll have to keep retouching? See page 220 for help when identifying your colour.

step 2

For the most accurate impression of what's inside the box, look at the colour chart on the side or back, rather than the model on the front. This will show you how far away from your natural colour the kit will take you.

step 3

Complete colour changes are best left to a salon professional. For the most flattering at-home results, avoid going more than two shades away from your natural hair colour. Any more than this and your new colour could clash with your skin tone, making you look flushed and ruddy, or tired and washed out.

Pro Tip

Grey hair has a coarser texture and can take longer to colour than other hues of hair, so if you have any predominantly grey areas, apply dye here first – and do buy a colouring kit especially designed for covering greys, which will take the difference in texture into account.

What's in the Box?

- **Permanent** Because they penetrate the hair shaft, permanent shades may fade slightly over time but won't wash out, meaning you'll have to continue colouring your hair or let the colour grow out when you get bored of it (though switching to a semi-permanent can help you grow out a permanent shade). Permanent shades are better at covering greys than semi-permanents, and often give a more dramatic result.

- **Semi-permanent** These deposit their pigments onto the surface of the hair and will wash out gradually over six to twelve washes, meaning you won't have to retouch your roots and won't be as committed to your new colour – although the more porous your hair, the longer the pigments can take to wash out.

- **Highlights or lowlights** These kits could contain both bleach and permanent colourants, and the tools needed for spot application, so you can choose exactly where you want to apply your colour.

- **Glosses and glazes** These add shine and a hint of semi-permanent colour, and will adjust your existing shade very slightly, to make it look brighter or softer, or give it a subtle new tone. You can also buy a clear gloss or glaze for boosting shine and vibrancy.

How to Suit Your Skin Tone

Choosing the right shade becomes less of a gamble once you've worked out whether your colouring is cool or warm. While there are always exceptions to the rule, these quick tests can help you decide.

step 1

Look at the veins on the inside of your wrists. If you have cool colouring, they will have a blue tone, but if your colouring is warm, they will have a greenish tinge (comparing with friends can help here).

step 2

If you have a cool complexion, your skin will have pink undertones. If your colouring is warm, its undertones will be peach or apricot.

step 3

Suiting silver jewellery often implies your colouring is cool. If you feel more comfortable in gold, you could fall into the warmer category.

step 4

If you have a cool complexion, avoid warm shades, which can make you seem sallow – these include anything with red, copper or golden undertones. If your complexion is warm, avoid colours with cool blue undertones, such as blue-black or ashy blonde shades.

Pro Tip

If you have your hair cut regularly at the same salon, your stylist shouldn't mind giving you advice about which shades would best suit your skin tone.

Applying Your Colour

All kits come with their own step-by-step instructions, as well as the tools you need to mix and apply them, but a few tips and tricks will help you get the most professional effect possible.

• A couple of dark towels, a pair of thin surgical gloves and some sectioning clips are helpful additions to the tools already in your kit.
• Before you start, smooth petroleum jelly along your hairline to prevent staining your skin. If you end up with a few smudges, try removing them with an alcohol-based skincare toner.
• Apply your colour to dry, well-brushed hair to avoid diluting the dye and make application easier. Always comb your colour through a few times with a wide-tooth comb to ensure even coverage.
• Read the leaflet that comes in the box from beginning to end at least twice, to avoid missing any key instructions.
• Sectioning your hair with clips can help you apply the dye thoroughly and evenly.
• Make sure your hair is saturated with dye, but never leave it on for longer than instructed. A timer with an alarm will help you avoid any accidents.

• Because they're older and potentially more porous, the tips of your hair can grab onto more colour than the mid-lengths. To avoid uneven results, work your dye through the rest of your hair first before reaching the ends.
• If you're lightening your hair, apply your dye to the roots last of all. This will create a subtly graded effect that looks more natural than colour that's exactly the same from root to tip.
• To retouch your colour without dyeing the rest of your hair, apply it just to your roots and then work the rest of the dye through your lengths and ends a few minutes before the processing time is up. Using a brush can make this easier. If your kit doesn't contain one, invest in a paintbrush of four to five centimetres in width.
• If your hair is naturally porous, or has been damaged by previous colouring treatments or chemical processing, it may take less time to dye than the instructions suggest.
• When your time is up, rinse until the water runs completely clear.
• Always use the intensive conditioner that comes with the colour (there's sometimes enough to use for the next few washes too). It will help to lock

in your colour, and give it an extra shot of softness and shine.

• If you're not keen on your new colour, wait for a couple of weeks before applying a new one, to give your hair time to recover.

• Using a moisturising mask during the week before you colour your hair can get it into the most resilient condition, decrease porosity and lead to a more even colour.

How to Complete a Strand Test

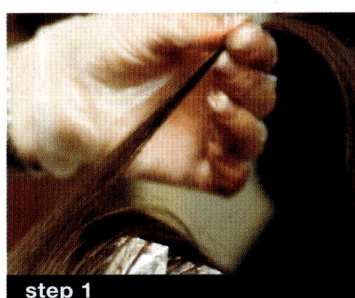

step 1

Choose a section that's near enough to your hairline to see against your skin tone, but far enough below the top layers to hide away if you decide not to colour the rest of your hair.

step 2

Clip the rest of your hair out of the way and follow the instructions on the box to mix your colour and dye the section. For a really accurate test, wipe off the dye halfway through the allotted time and blot your hair dry with a towel to see how the colour has taken. You may find this is all the time you'll need to get the result you want. If not, reapply the dye and leave on for the remaining minutes.

step 3

When your time is up and you've removed the dye and dried off the section on a low heat, look at the section near a window, so you can see what the colour looks like in natural light. If you like what you see, go ahead and colour the rest.

Pro Tip

If you're using a kit or colour you've never tried before, complete a strand test first by colouring a one-centimetre section of hair.

Colour Theory

Identifying Your Natural Colour

An international system is used in salons to identify the level of darkness of your hair, 1 being the darkest (black) and 10 being the lightest (blonde). When using home colouring, match your hair (just the re-growth if previously coloured) to the hair colour chart below that most closely resembles the **darkness** of your hair colour. Your colour should not necessarily represent the **tone**, which could be warm (red), cool (ash) or neutral, but the degree of lightness or darkness. Knowing this you can work out which colour you would like your hair to be. The more you stray from your natural hair colour, the harder it is to maintain. Stylists recommend staying within three shades of your natural colour.

Tones

1—Ash
2—Iridescent or violet (brands differ)
3—Gold
4—Red
5—Mahogany
6—Violet
7—Brunette or green (brands differ)
8—Pearl

Natural Hair Colour Level System

Black	Dark Brown	Brown	Medium Brown	Light Brown	Dark Blonde	Blonde	Medium Blonde	Light Blonde	Lightest Blonde
1	2	3	4	5	6	7	8	9	10

Red	Red/ Orange	Orange	Orange/ Yellow	Yellow/ Orange	Yellow	Pale Yellow

Underlying Pigments

Colouring Demystified

When you have your hair coloured at the salon, stylists use a number method to make sure you get a hair colour that suits you.

Using the Natural Hair Colour Level System diagram (above), a stylist would first identify the depth and shade of your colour and keep note of the number. By identifying this colour first they can show you the new shade that would suit you. The second number that a stylist would use

refers to the tone of the colour. This can be graded between 1 and 8 (see Tones box, above). There is sometimes a third number, if the hair has a secondary tone. This will enhance or neutralise the different tones in the hair.

For example, if you have a natural base of a '5' light brown (with orange pigment, see diagram), and you want to lighten your hair two shades to a '7' blond (yellow/orange pigment) the stylist could choose to keep the natural warmth in your tone by using a colour '7'. However, they may think about enhancing the golden shade coming through by using a depth of a no. '7' colour with a no. '3' (gold) tone. To neutralise the golden shade and have a more natural tone they may use a no. '7' but with a no. '1' (ash) tone. This works because the ash (a cool tone) neutralises the yellow/orange (both warm tones).

These numbers are also often on the side of shop-bought colours, although the keys vary so make sure you read the packaging carefully.

Corrective Hair Colour

The colour wheel consists of three primary colours: red, blue and yellow. It also consists of three secondary colours: green, orange and violet. Each primary and secondary colour has an opposite colour. It's important to know these opposites, as stylists use them to correct unwanted colour or tone in the hair.

If a client had bright yellow hair, the stylist would have to neutralise the yellow with violet to create a more natural tone.

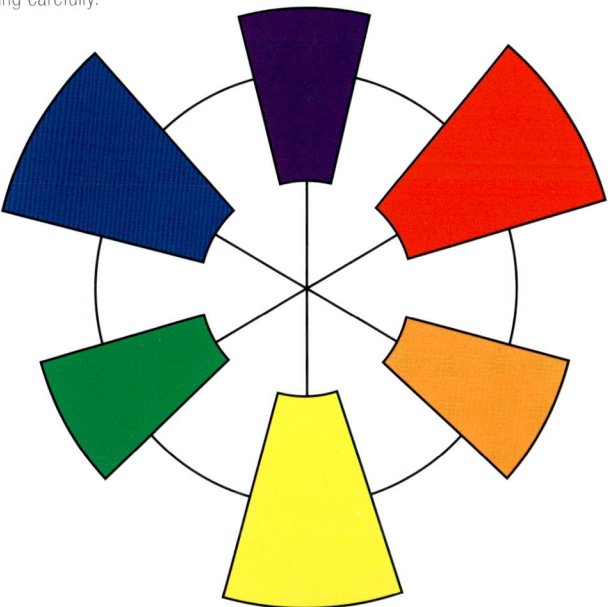

COLOUR	NEUTRALISING COLOUR
RED	GREEN
YELLOW	VIOLET
BLUE	ORANGE
GREEN	RED
VIOLET	YELLOW
ORANGE	BLUE

Pro Tip

Hair that is highlighted with bleach can sometimes remove too much pigment from the hair, resulting in a colour that may be too blonde. The most effective way to tone the abrasive hair colour is to use a colour gloss or toner to add or deposit colour back into the hair. Toners can also be used on brunette hair.

Chapter 8

AT THE SALON

Explaining exactly what you want to a stylist can feel daunting, but knowing how to communicate with the professionals means you're more likely to walk out of the salon with the look you've always wanted.

UNDERSTANDING FACE SHAPES

Some cuts can flatter the structure of your face, while others may accentuate it unfavourably. Here are a few terms that your stylist may use when explaining why the look you want won't work with your bone structure, or when suggesting an alternative approach.

Square jaw

The strong lines of a square jaw often need softening, which means framing the face with layers, gently graduated cuts and feathered and razored ends, rather than exposing it with blunt lines, harsh crops and sharp angles.

Broad forehead

As with a square jaw, blunt edges and sharp angles can accentuate a wide forehead, so your stylist will probably avoid a solid fringe and go for something softly feathered, to frame your face in a more flattering way.

Long forehead

A fringe can help break up the expanse of an overly long forehead. Layers can create softness, as can styles with fullness at the side rather than height on top or too much length.

Round face

A side-swept fringe, long layers or height at the crown can lengthen your face and draw attention to your cheekbones, whereas a short crop, a straight, wide fringe or a chin-length, voluminous bob will only accentuate the fullness of your face.

Heart-shaped face

The top-heavy proportions of a heart-shaped face can be balanced out with a short, soft, choppy crop, or chin-length layers. Your stylist will probably avoid a blunt fringe, or any style with a lot of height.

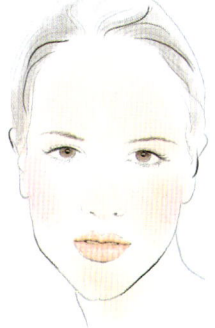

Oval face

Not too round and not too square, the balanced proportions of an oval face make this the most versatile shape of all. There's little that won't suit you, unless your face is slightly long, in which case, a fringe or an off-centre parting will break up the illusion of length.

SALON TERMINOLOGY

When it comes to getting the look you want, knowing how to communicate with your hairdresser is half the battle. While any good stylist will talk to you in a way you'll understand, it doesn't hurt to recognise a few key terms, or to be armed with a healthy dose of salon confidence.

Cutting Terminology

Bevelled edge	The ends are cut at a slight angle rather than at a blunt 90 degrees, so the hair turns slightly under or outwards. A bevelled edge can help the hair curve under, or add a softer, rounder finish.
Blunt cut	The ends are cut to the same length at a 90-degree angle. This gives a harder edge and more classic definition to your style.
Crown	The area at the very top of the head. However, when stylists talk about creating volume at the crown, they're usually referring to the area a little further towards the back of the head, diagonally up and back from the ear.
Disconnection	Individual sections are randomly cut and layered, but create an overall shape.
Dusting	To remove a minimal amount of hair from the ends.
Feathering	Cutting diagonally into the hair to soften straight lines and blunt ends. This popular technique can be created by using scissors or razors.
Freehand	A method of cutting hair using scissors only and without a comb to hold hair in place. Defines and personalises your style and is great for hairlines and fringes.

Graduated	When a cut is graduated, top layers of the hair are longer and lie on the shorter layers of the hair beneath it; this can create shape and volume in certain areas.
Layering	The top layers of hair are shorter than the bottom layers. Layering the hair creates depth and movement and can tame thick or coarse tresses.
Movement	A feeling of depth and texture is created by cutting (slicing or razoring) or colouring techniques, so the hair looks tousled or fluid rather than stiff and solid.
Overdirection	When sections of hair are directed further over the head rather than straight out from the head. This method works well with long layers and maintains volume in desired areas.
Point cutting	Snipping into dry hair with the points of the scissors to fine-tune a finished cut, create texture, remove weight and soften a look.
Razoring (slicing)	Cutting into the hair with a blade to reduce bulk and excess weight, gives a softer, feathery effect, and helps create movement.
Scissor over comb	Normally a barbering technique, this is when the comb is used to elevate segments of the hair, which are then cut by the scissors. Ideal for shorter hairstyles and for men's cuts.
Shattered	A cut or outline that's been heavily cut into (and often razored) to create a shaggy or choppy effect with no blunt lines.
Texture	Any effect that doesn't look blunt, sleek or poker-straight. This can refer to the natural character of the hair (waves or curls, for example), or an effect that's created by cutting techniques such as layering, razoring or point cutting, or by styling techniques such as scrunching or rough drying.
Texturising	Cutting into the ends of the hair using point cutting, razoring or thinning techniques, to remove weight and add texture and movement.
Thinning	Removes weight from the hair. Can be done anywhere along the hair shaft from root to tip using thinning scissors or razors.
Undercutting	Cutting layers underneath shorter than the layers on top reduces bulk, helps thick hair to hang smoothly, creates a style that is easier to curl under at the ends and is great for fashion cuts.

Cuts Glossary

Bob	A style that's cut to the same length all the way around – usually between the ear and shoulder.
Bob A-line	This bob style is shorter at the back and longer at the front (with or without a fringe).
Bob graduated	This has a bevelled effect through the back, either by graduation or layering.
Concave layers	Recognised by the inwardly curving silhouette created by the layering, or by the base line of the style. The modern-day bob with the sharply turned curvature between the short back length and the longer front length is a good example of concave layering.
Convex layers	Recognised by their outwardly curving line, especially in area shaped by layers, convex layers can have various degrees of arching in the base line. Round layers are always convex layers.
Crop	A short style that sits close to the head. It is often referred to as pixie cut, gamine or boyish style.
One-length cut	Long hair cut all to the same length at 0 degrees, without lifting or layering. A shorter version would be the bob.
Round layers	An evenly layered cut when all the hair is held directly out from the head and cut at 90 degrees. Cut in a round shape this distributes weight evenly through the hair and can be very flattering on most face shapes.
Square layers	A layered, face-framing cut with a lot of volume and soft, feathery ends. Hair is cut at one level directly up or out from the head in a boxy shape that maintains weight at the base.

Colour Terminology

Balayage	A French technique that involves hand painting highlights onto the hair for a less uniform effect.
Fashion colour	Involves advanced colouring techniques, usually by adding bright or vibrant flashes of colour on prelightened hair, that represent current fashion trends, and complement or enhance the cut.
Full head	When highlights or lowlights are applied throughout the hair, from the upper to the lower layers. Great if you like to wear your hair in many different styles and want a full coverage.
Half head	Fewer highlights or lowlights are applied and they are concentrated in the upper layers of the hair, from the ear line upwards, rather than all the way through. This is cheaper and quicker than a full head but gives pretty much the same effect.
Parting highlights	When highlights or lowlights are placed along the parting by weaving or slicing. Colour lays over the top of your finished style.
Semi	A semi-permanent colour that's applied from root to tip. Ideal for colour changes, adding shine and a different tone, and covering up to 75 per cent grey hair. Usually lasts around six to eight weeks.
Tint	A permanent colour that's applied from the scalp to the ends. Ideal for colour changes, adding shine and a different tone, and covering up to 100 per cent grey hair. Lasts until the hair grows out.
Toner	An all-over semi-colour applied to hair that's been bleached, highlighted or coloured, to help fine-tune and personalise the desired shade.
T-section highlights	When highlights or lowlights are placed along the parting and around the front of the face to resemble a 'T' shape.

Colour Glossary

Ashy	Blonde shades with cool undertones.
Bleach	Hair bleaching is the process of removing the pigment from the hair strand. It can be used to prelighten, highlight or create fashion colours.
Brassy tones	Harsh and unwanted yellowy-gold tones in blonde shades and highlights.
Cool	A term used to describe a skin tone or hair colour with blue/violet/green undertones.
Peroxide	Used as an activator for most colours including tint, semi and bleach. The peroxide is used in an alkaline solution, which opens the hair shaft to allow the colour to enter.
Prelighten	Prelightening is sometimes required to achieve a desired colour. When hair is lightened it produces warm or red and yellow undertones. These may be enhanced or neutralised using toners.
Highlights	When one or more lighter tones are painted onto the hair in thin or thick strands (weaved) or slices, for a streaked or natural effect rather than a solid colour.
Lowlights	When darker tones are painted onto the hair for a streaked or natural rather than a solid effect. These are sometimes combined with highlights to create even more depth and movement.
Lift	To lighten a hair colour by one or more shades.
Patch test	A test to ensure that a client's skin won't react badly to the chemicals in a hair colour. A small amount of colour is applied to the client's skin (normally on the inside of the arm) and covered with a plaster. The test is carried out a day or two before the appointment and usually applies to permanent tints or semi-permanent colours, as highlights and lowlights don't touch the scalp.
Weave	When highlights or lowlights are weaved into the hair with a pintail comb it leaves some natural colour, which gives a more natural effect.
Slices	Highlights or lowlights that are slightly wider than usual. They allow more colour placement than weaved highlights by colouring whole strips of hair at a time.

Virgin hair	Hair that has never been coloured or chemically processed.
Warm	A term used to describe a skin tone or hair colour with yellow, orange or red undertones.

Texturising Treatments

Altering the texture of your hair with a chemical salon treatment can help control frizz, reduce drying time or simply allow you to achieve the kind of looks that just don't work with your natural hair type. Straightening processes are by far the most popular – not only to reverse unwanted waves and curls, but also to boost shine and manageability in all hair types, leaving you with hair that falls obediently into place after every wash.

Japanese Hair Straightening	This chemical relaxing treatment works on almost every hair type (although Afro-Caribbean hair can be hard to treat), and leaves hair poker-straight and frizz free, with no need for daily blow-drying or straightening. The process can take up to four hours of salon time, during which a collagen, keratin and silk protein solution is allowed to penetrate the follicles, before the hair is set with a hot iron. Results are permanent, although top-up treatments will be required every four to nine months if you want to maintain the look, as new hair growth will revert to its original texture.
Brazilian Blow-dry	Unlike the Japanese system, this semi-permanent straightening treatment washes out over time, but will still leave your hair sleek, manageable and frizz-proof without daily blow-drying or straightening. Processing takes from one to four hours, during which the hair is coated with a keratin solution and straightened with hot irons. Results last for around three to four months, during which time hair slowly reverts to its natural texture.
Relaxing	Straightening treatments designed to restructure Afro-Caribbean hair types use strong alkaline chemicals to break down the bonds between the hair proteins, which allows the stylist to set the hair into a new shape. When the chemicals are neutralised, the protein bonds reform, and the hair permanently takes on the new texture. Results grow out over time so top-up treatments are needed every eight to twelve weeks. These treatments can be carried out at home, but as the strong chemicals can leave your hair damaged and weakened, salon treatments are always preferable.

Salon Confidence

Finding a new stylist or experimenting with a new look can feel daunting – but be brave! Here are a few useful tips to bear in mind when you next step out of your comfort zone.

- A good salon will always give you a consultation free of charge, whether you're trying out a new stylist or just thinking about a new look. If a potential stylist won't take ten minutes to talk to you about your hair before you make an appointment, move on to another salon.
- If you're looking for a new stylist, speak to the salon reception about what you want and find out whether the salon has someone who specialises in that area, or whether there's someone who really enjoys creating the kind of cut and colour you want. Alternatively, ask friends if they can recommend someone, or if you see someone on the street with great hair, ask where they had it done.
- Pictures speak louder than words, but if you're showing your stylist an image of a cut or colour you really love, try to work out what it is you like so much about it. If that exact cut or colour won't work with your face shape or hair type, your stylist may be able to suggest a different approach.

- Be honest with your stylist about how often you can afford to come back to the salon, and how long you'll spend styling your hair every day. This will help you get a cut or colour you'll be able to maintain at home without too much expense.
- If you like wearing your hair up, tell your stylist so they can make sure they leave you with enough length and weight to create your favourite styles.
- Good stylists will tell you what they're going to do to your hair before they start cutting. If yours doesn't, ask them to explain first. This will also help you to make sure they really understand what you've asked for.
- Always ask your stylist what your new cut will look like if you allow it to dry naturally. If you're not planning to blow-dry or straighten your hair every day, you may end up with a completely different look at home. Dry cutting is a great technique for this as the stylist can see how your hair sits naturally and can create a style from there.

- When your stylist has finished cutting and started drying and styling, ask what they're doing and which styling products they're using, so you can recreate the effect at home. This is also a good time to ask for alternative styling suggestions, so you can get different looks from the same cut.
- A stylist you see regularly will usually trim your fringe for free – just don't spring it on them. Ask when the salon's quietest times are, and call that morning to say you'll be dropping in.
- If you don't like a new cut or colour, do tell your stylist. A good salon will want to keep you happy. If you don't think you've got what you asked for, the salon should offer to fix it for free. If you did get what you asked for but just don't like it, your stylist should be able to suggest a way to tweak the style to make you more comfortable, even if you have to pay for another appointment.

- Hair is always a work in progress. As well as thinking about how you'll look when you leave the salon, the best stylists think about how your cut or colour could be developed over the next few months, seasons or even years. This is one of the best arguments for sticking with the same stylist.
- If you feel stuck in a rut and are thinking about trying a new look or style, ask your stylist first for ideas or inspiration. If you fancy trying a new stylist get a friend to recommend you to someone they know and trust. Your stylist won't mind, as change can be good – and they'll always welcome you back.

Chapter 9

TROUBLESHOOTING

From falling flat by lunchtime to splitting at the ends, when your hair's not behaving exactly as it should or you can't put your finger on why a style's not working, this is the chapter to turn to.

TROUBLESHOOTING

Hair falling flat? Scalp feeling dry? Here are a few common hair-care and styling problems and some simple ways to solve them.

Problem	Cause	Why	Solution
Flaky Scalp	Product build-up	Shampoo, conditioner and styling products can build up on your scalp and hair and begin to flake off.	Make sure you're using the right shampoo and conditioner for your hair type, and not applying too much styling product. Use a clarifying shampoo once a week, and rinse your hair thoroughly after washing it.
	Dandruff	Stress, poor diet and hormones can all lead to a bacterial imbalance on the surface of the scalp, which in turn leads to an increase in skin shedding and sebum production, causing a build-up of oily flakes.	An antifungal or antimicrobial shampoo will help control the problem, but do speak to a pharmacist rather than just pick something from the shelf, and try to think about which aspects of your lifestyle may be contributing to the problem. If symptoms don't decrease in a couple of months, see your doctor, who may be able to refer you to a dermatologist.

Problem	Cause	Why	Solution
	Psoriasis	This itching, flaking condition (sometimes accompanied with crumbling nails and red patches elsewhere on the face and body) is a genetic and recurring skin disease that ranges from mild to serious and can be triggered by stress.	See your doctor for diagnosis and treatment, which will usually include special hair-care products and oral medication.
Greasy Hair	Over-stimulating your oil glands.	Brushing and massaging too strenuously, washing your hair in overly hot water and using harsh hair-care products can all stimulate your scalp into producing too much oil, in a bid to protect itself.	Keep massage to a minimum, avoid brushing too close to your scalp and try switching to a milder shampoo.
	Product overload	Oil-based styling products, masks and conditioners (or any that are too heavy for your hair type) can leave your hair looking greasy and flat.	Look for oil-free styling products and lighter hair-care formulations, and avoid applying products and conditioner to your roots. Try a spritz of dry shampoo to keep your roots feeling fresh, and avoid fiddling with your hair too much, as it can pick up a surprising amount of dirt and oil from your fingertips through the day.

Problem	Cause	Why	Solution
Split Ends	Wear and tear from daily styling or chemical treatments.	Vigorous brushing, overprocessing and the misuse of heated styling tools can tear the hair, especially at the ends, which are older and weaker than the roots and mid-lengths.	Always use a comb rather than a brush when your hair is wet, and remove tangles and knots by starting at the bottom and working your way up. Keep heated styling to a minimum, always use heat-protective styling products and use a protein-based hair mask regularly. Have your hair trimmed every six to eight weeks, to prevent the split from travelling further up the hair shaft.
Weak, Dull Hair with Split Ends	Growing your hair too long.	The longer hair gets, the older and more fragile the ends become, and the further its natural oils have to travel to keep the lengths lubricated. Some hair types aren't strong enough to cope, and can look dull and lifeless.	Have your hair trimmed every six to eight weeks to keep the ends strong and healthy, talk to your stylist about your optimum length and read the guide to healthy hair nutrition on page 26.
Breakages Further Up the Hair Shaft	The factors that cause split ends can all contribute (see above), as can poor nutrition and pulling your hair back too tightly with hair elastics.	Poorly fed hair can become brittle and weak, hair elastics can snag your hair and the constant tension created by tight updos can lead to breakages.	Read the guide to healthy hair nutrition on page 26. Use smooth and seamless hair elastics without metal bobbles (which can catch on your hair) and try not to pull your hair back too tightly, or wear it up every day.

Problem	Cause	Why	Solution
Frizzy Hair	Humid environments	In a damp or humid environment hair can soak up moisture like a sponge, especially if it's dry or damaged. The hair will then swell and twist, leading to a frizzy, wavy or curly texture.	Keep your hair as hydrated as possible with the correct hair care and regular treatments. Look for frizz-proof styling products and consider having your hair permanently straightened. Also consider a longer style if appropriate, as the extra weight will pull your hair down and prevent it from frizzing quite as much.
	Overbrushing naturally curly hair.	The bristles can cause tension and static, leading to a fluffy texture.	Apply a leave-in conditioner while your hair is still damp after washing, and allow it to air-dry, or use a diffuser and keep your dryer on a low heat setting. Once dry, try not to overstyle or fiddle with your hair, as this can encourage the frizz to return.
	Damage caused by daily wear and tear, sun exposure or chemical treatments.	These can all damage the protective cuticle layer that keeps the surface of your hair looking smooth and sleek.	Use styling products with UV protection, switch to a milder shampoo, keep heated styling techniques to a minimum and use regular moisturising treatments.
Flyaway Hair	A dry environment	Climates that lack moisture can dehydrate your hair and lead to a fluffy, static texture.	Switch to a moisturising shampoo and conditioner, and use a natural bristle brush, which will help distribute your natural oils from root to tip. Also try leave-in conditioners and UV-protective styling products.

Problem	Cause	Why	Solution
Dull Hair	Not rinsing properly after washing and conditioning.	Shampoo's cleansing properties are activated by water, so insufficient rinsing will leave your hair coated with dirt, shampoo suds and possibly conditioner too.	Rinse until the water running through the ends of your hair is completely clear.
	Poor diet	A lack of essential fatty acids can lead to a deficiency in the natural oils that keep your hair protected and conditioned.	Increase your intake of oily fish, nuts, seeds and avocados.
	Product build-up	Shampoo, conditioner and styling products can build up on your hair, leaving it sticky and lacklustre.	Check you're using the correct shampoo, conditioner and styling products for your hair type, and that you're not applying too much of them. Use a clarifying shampoo once a week, rinse your hair thoroughly after washing and clean your combs and hairbrushes once a week in a mild solution of shampoo and water.
	A damaged cuticle layer	In order to reflect light and create the appearance of healthy, shiny hair, the protective cuticles on the surface of the hair shaft should all lie flat. Many factors can leave this layer ruffled and damaged, including daily wear and tear and harsh chemical processing.	Switch to a milder shampoo and a moisturising conditioner. Avoid rubbing your cuticles the wrong way by carefully blotting your hair dry rather than rubbing it, and always directing the hot air of your dryer down the hair shaft from root to tip. Keep heated styling tools to a minimum, and redress the damage done by chemical processing with regular treatments.

Problem	Cause	Why	Solution
Dry Hair	A harsh hair-care routine	Washing your hair too often, or with harsh detergents, and exposing your hair to high temperatures on a daily basis can strip your hair of its protective oils, weaken the cuticle layer and sap moisture.	Switch to a milder shampoo (and make sure you're not using too much of it) and try a richer conditioner. Use heat-protective styling products and take time off from heated styling tools whenever possible.
	A dehydrating environment	Dry, hot climates and centrally heated environments can strip your hair of moisture.	Use moisturising shampoo and regular conditioning treatments, and keep heated styling tools to a minimum.
	Swimming	The chemical content and pH balance of chlorinated water can strip your hair of natural oils and moisture, while washing and drying it after every swim can exacerbate the damage.	Coat your hair with conditioner and/or wear a watertight swim cap, or try rinsing your hair before getting into the pool, as the wetter your hair is, the less pool water it will soak up. Use a mild shampoo or one designed for swimmers, a rich conditioner and regular treatments.
	Chemical processing	The chemical solutions used in coloring and texturising treatments can compromise your cuticle layer and sap moisture from the hair.	Repair as much damage as possible with regular moisturising masks and cut down on the amount of bleach you're exposing your hair to. If you already have a fair base colour, consider switching to a high lift tint, as these are usually gentler than anything that contains bleach.

Problem	Cause	Why	Solution
Limp Hair	Styling product overload	Products that are overapplied, too heavy for your hair type or applied too near to the roots can weigh your hair down.	Follow the guides to choosing and using the right styling products on pages 34–43. Try a volumising mousse, and backcomb gently at the roots to create body and lift.
	The wrong cut	Too much length or weight can drag hair down and knock out its natural body.	Ask your stylist to help you consider a shorter or layered cut, but avoid too many layers if your hair is thin or fine.
A Style Not Lasting	Prepping your hair with too much or too little product.	Staying power needs to be built into your hair right from the start with a product such as mousse or thickening spray. Too little and you'll never get your style to stay in place; too much and your hair will flop under its own weight.	Follow the guide to establishing your hair type on page 18, and choose your styling products accordingly from the guide on pages 34–43. Apply a small amount to start with and add more, until you can gauge how much your hair needs.
	Too much hair	Hair can sometimes be too long or thick to hold an updo, and will collapse under its own weight.	If you have your heart set on a particular style, speak to your stylist. They may be able to trim away just enough length or weight to make the style workable.

Problem	Cause	Why	Solution
Hair Loss	Pregnancy	During pregnancy, a larger number of follicles than usual enter the resting phase, so less hair falls out, creating the appearance of thicker hair and more body. A few months after pregnancy this extra hair begins to shed.	Recognise that you're not shedding anything you can't afford to lose, and that your hair only seems thin in relation to the temporary fullness you benefitted from during pregnancy. If you feel you are suffering from anything beyond this, it could be caused by a nutritional deficiency. Read the guide to healthy hair nutrition on page 26. If the problem persists, see your doctor for advice. There are many other reasons for hair loss (also known as alopecia), ranging from genetic male pattern baldness, to stress, nutrition deficiencies, or health problems such as a thyroid imbalance. If you have any worries, contact your doctor for advice.

Problem	Cause	Why	Solution
Colour Fading Too Quickly	Using the wrong hair care.	Harsh shampoos, ineffective conditioners and some volumising hair-care formulations can leave the cuticles on the surface of the hair open. This allows colour particles to leach out and colour-dulling impurities to get in. A rougher surface also creates less shine, which can make your colour appear less intense.	Use shampoos, conditioners and masks formulated for coloured hair.
	Washing too often, or using dandruff shampoos.	Overwashing or using medicated shampoo can strip colour from your hair.	Switch to a milder shampoo, or alternate with every other wash.
	Exposure to sunlight or chemically treated swimming pools.	UV light and chlorinated water can bleach your hair, as well as damaging the cuticles, making it less able to retain colour particles.	Use UV-protective styling products and wear a scarf or hat in strong sunlight. Keep your hair well moisturised with regular treatments, to maintain strength and resilience. Wear a watertight swim cap and, for extra protection, coat the hair underneath with conditioner.
	Choosing the wrong colour.	The further from your natural shade, the harder it is to maintain vibrancy and strength.	Stay within two or three shades of your natural hair colour.

Problem	Cause	Why	Solution
Highlights Look Green or Brassy	Using the wrong hair care.	Not using specific aftercare products for blonde shades.	There are specific shampoos and conditioners on the market to help enhance blond shades and keep them looking fresh and natural. These products are usually blue or purple in colour and should be used one-to-two times a week in between your regular wash.
	Swimming in chlorinated pool water.	Copper in water. Copper and chlorine have a positive charge, skin and hair have a negative one, so the copper builds up on the hair causing a temporary stain.	Before swimming, wet hair well, apply a deep conditioner, and wear a swimming hat. Hair can't absorb water if it is already wet. After swimming, rinse hair thoroughly and towel dry. Shampoo with a 'swimmers shampoo' – it has a lower pH. If your hair has been stained, an edible tomato sauce or juice can act as an antioxidant and will remove the green colour. Apply to hair and leave for up for thirty minutes before rinsing.

RESOURCES

General Hair Help

Asos: www.asos.com
Beautique: www.beautique.com
HQ Hair: www.hqhair.com
Look Fantastic: www.lookfantastic.com
Space NK: www.spacenk.co.uk
Sephora: www.sephora.com

Products

GHD: www.ghdhair.com / www.ghdhair.com.au
L'Oréal: www.loreal.co.uk / www.loreal.com.au
Tigi: www.tigihaircare.com
Fekkai: www.sephora.com
Sebastien: www.sebastienprofessional.com
John Frieda: www.johnfrieda.co.uk / www.johnfrieda.com
Trésemmé: www.tresemme.co.uk / www.tresemme.com.au

Equipment

Matador combs and brushes available at www.hairscissors.co.uk / www.pak-super.com
Denman: www.denmanbrush.com
Babyliss: www.babylissus.co.uk / www.babylissus.com

INDEX

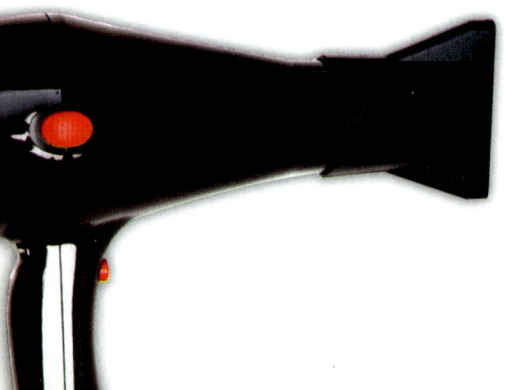

ACKNOWLEDGEMENTS

With thanks to the models on the shoot: Tom Bennett, Tabby Brown, Hannie Lyngved, Rachel Jenkins, Ling Pham, Vanessa Portelli, Anna Slater and Nicole Tristan.

Quintet and the authors would like to thank Andrew at Andrew Brown Hair Salon; Owen at Blu Fusion Models; Karen at Capital Hair and Beauty Supplies; Preeya Varsani and Lucy Armitt at The Communications Store; Caroline Pugh at Kilpatrick PR; Rebecca Filmer, Emma Scott, Nicky Thompson, and Claire Nash at L'Oréal UK; Carol at Needhams Models; Ashley at Pure PR; Natalie Hellon at Shine Communication for GHD; Philip Donaldson at P&G Salon Professionals for Wella Professionals; David Murphy at Studio Arch 63; Alexandra Sananes at Talk PR; and Karleen Smith at Tigi International.

PICTURE CREDITS